© **William S. Page 2020**

All rights reserved. No part of this publication may be reproduced, stored in a retrieval system, or transmitted in any form or by any means, electronic, mechanical, photocopying, recording, or otherwise, without the prior written permission of the author.

Printed in United States of America

Contents

Chapter 1..**6**

Understanding Elementor Page Builder

The History of Elementor

Elementor Community

How does Elementor Plugin Developers make Money?

The Contents of Elementor Page Builder

Chapter 2..**18**

WordPress, Elementor Templates and Benefits of Building a Website with Elementor

Using WordPress comes in three flavors

The Components of WordPress Screen Options

Elementor Templates

The Benefits of Building Websites with Elementor

Chapter 3..39

Choosing a Domain Name and Hosting

What you should know in Choosing Domain name

Domain Name Registration

Practical: Step-by-Step Guide in Registering your Domain Name

Chapter 4..62

Installing WordPress and Account Setup through Control Panel

A Step-by-step Guide on how to Install WordPress and Continue with Building of your Website

What will You do if after Installation your Website does not Load?

Chapter 5..87

New Theme Installation

Chapter 6..103

Building Website Pages

What are the Pages we will be Creating?

Step by Step Guide in Creation Home Page with Elementor and Adding it to Main Menu

Step by Step Guide in Adding the Home Page as a Main Menu Item

Step by Step Guide in Creating "Contact" Page

Step by Step Guide in Adding the Contact Page as a Main Menu Item

Step by Step Guide in Creating "About" Page

Step by Step Guide in Adding the Created "About" Page to Navigation Menu as Menu Item

Chapter 7..127

Footer Design with Elementor

How to build the Footer Contents with Elementor

Next: Designing the Footer Template After Import

Building Social Media Links at Footer with Elementor

Chapter 8...147

How to Build a Restaurant and Café Website with Elementor

What is a Restaurant and Café Website?

Step by Step Guide in Choosing the Right Template for the Restaurant Website

Chapter 9..159

Guide on how to Build E-Commerce Website Using Elementor

In Summary: Setting Up an Ecommerce Website from Choosing Domain Name to use of Elementor

Installing and Activating Elementor for E-Commerce Website

How to Build the Homepage of your E-Commerce Site with Elementor

Guide on how to insert or change your E-commerce Site Title, Tagline and Logo

Chapter 1

Understanding Elementor Page Builder

Elementor is a powerful page builder with powerful features. It was developed with stunning tools. Since the advent of elementor plugin, many things have changed in the world of website building. People have more freedom to build many kinds of websites with the tool.

As of the time of publishing this book, elementor has over 5,000,000+ professionals who built better sites with it. In this book, I will try as much as I can to guide you on how to build great kinds of websites with elementor page builder. This includes blog sites, business websites, e-commerce websites and portfolio sites. You will be happy you got this book at the end of this teaching. If you have any issue as you build your website with elementor, do not hesitate to write to me through my email on the last page of this book. I will respond to you as fast as possible.

The History of Elementor

The beautiful plugin, elementor, was created and developed in the year 2016. It was a hard work put together by developers. This hard work of these team of software developers at the end gave birth to what many website builders are making use to create beautiful online brands today.

When the software was created, it did not have many users. As the company began to advertise and create more popularity among internet users, many who have website building skills decided to give it a try. Today, almost everyone who wants to build a website wants to build with elementor page builder. It lives you with many options.

On the hand, elementor is evolving everyday with better features and functions. The developers are working on its compatibility with different devices like tablets and mobile phones. As of June 2020, I could not be able to make some designs on my website with my android phone using elementor. The two were not compactible. But as of August 08, 2020, the challenge became history. The team of elementor developers fixed that and made the plugin compatible with android devices in terms of using such phones for design. The men are really working.

Elementor is an open-source, GPLv3 licensed offering its platform both as free and premium. Since its creation in 2016, it has been used in over 180 countries in the world. It is a fast-growing plugin.

The three co-founders of Elementor are Yoni Luksenberg, Ariel Klikstein, and Kfir Biton. But the two major founders are Yoni Luksenberg and Ariel Klikstein in 2016. Among the two, Yoni Luksenberg is the CEO.

When they began to work on the elementor project, it was not an easy task. But they kept going, and today elementor is one of the recent most cherished page builders used by bloggers and professional website designers.

Which country owns elementor or where was it built? Elementor Ltd. is an Israeli software company. The Israel tech professionals are the brain behind it. This gives good credit to the country.

In terms of designing with the software, you do that by employing the drag and drop technique. This make the design easy to carry out. The headquarter of Elementor Ltd is in Ramat Gan, Israel.

What about the languages that elementor accepts? As of July 2020, elementor works in 50 languages globally.

In elementor's first round of institutional funding, the company raised $15M from Lightspeed Venture Partners. Lightspeed Venture Partners is an American venture capital firm focusing on early stage investments in the enterprise technology and consumer space.

Elementor Community

Besides Elementor's easy to use, it has a strong community where you can get help, a piece of advice, and some support. The community is made up of both people who need support and experts in elementor related issues. It makes working as a website designer with elementor page builder interesting.

Let us assume that you are building an e-commerce website using elementor for your design. And at a point you run into technical issue which you cannot resolve. You then search through search engine but cannot get an article that specifically tackles the issue. Taking that complain to Elementor Community can get that issue resolved within few minutes.

When you post concerning that issue, you will get replies from community members. Some have years of experience in the use of the plugin and can willingly give you answers to what you are seeking for. Also, staff of the company can come in to provide the solution if the issue is so technical.

To access the community of elementor, visit www.elementor.com and select the menu bar, then select community.

Features ▼

Pricing

Resources ▼

Community

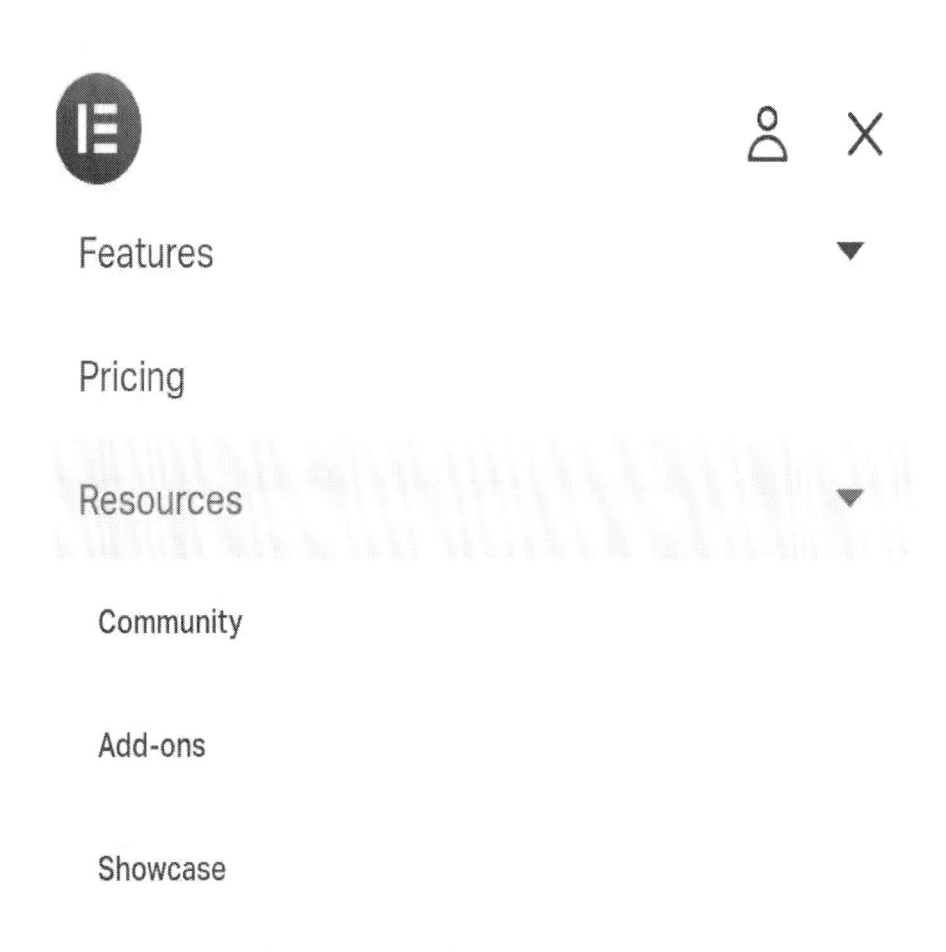

Add-ons

Showcase

Fig 1: Guide on how to get to elementor community

Also, you can decide to access community of elementor by direct link. The direct link is https://elementor.com/community/. This link was active as of August 3, 2020 because the company may decide to change the link any time they want to do so. To be a member of the community, you are to create an account with them when you visit the page. You can also join their social media community platforms. This includes Facebook, Twitter, Instagram and the rest. These individual platforms are made up with people that want to learn something new as get clarification on the page builder.

How does Elementor Plugin Developers make Money?

Sometimes users of elementor wonder how the developers make money from the plugins and add-on. But on the other way, what makes a company invest millions of dollars inside is a cool business. You may not see it as a public business the way physical business owners sample their products to buyers, but this is a coded business.

The way elementor makes their money is not that far from how other developers make their money as well. In summary, elementor makes their money through the following way:

- Elementor makes money from their Premium version

- They make money from sells of widgets

- Elementor makes money through their team of website builders and marketers.

Elementor offers both free and pro versions of their plugins. Some website builders and designers who want to give their websites exceptional design can go as far as buying pro version of the plugin. The prices vary depending on the functions integrated in each.

Some pro elementor users pay $49 annual, others $99 while there is another subscription of $199 in a year. Imagine out of the over 5 million users of elementor, average of 500,000 uses the Pro version in a year, it is a whole lot of money.

That is a cool business. So, if you see elementor in massive advertising through many platforms, they know what they are doing. They are running business of millions of dollars which with time will turn billions of dollars. So, the company makes cool money.

Elementor allows users to pay for some widgets they want to use on their websites for their designs. Maybe you are making use of the elementor free version and wants to buy just the slider widget to use it to add slider to your website, you can buy it. That is different from paying for a complete pro version of elementor. As you buy this slider, you can just design with it since that's what you need to add to your free version.

Furthermore, I listed that another way the company makes their money is through their team of website builders. Maybe you need someone that can build a website for your company for you, elementor has many who work as professional website builders.

Fig 1.1: Screenshot of elementor team of experts

All you need is to offer the project to elementor and they hand over the work to the professional. At the end of the project, elementor and the expert shares revenue and make money. The same applies when you need someone to help you promote your brand. They can help you get the job done.

The Contents of Elementor Page Builder

In one of the chapters to come, I will be discussing the installation and activation of elementor page builder. But I want you to know about the components of this tool before you start working with it.

Site Logo Widget (Pro)

The Site Logo widget is a dynamic widget that displays the Site Logo that was assigned in the WordPress Customizer. The Site Logo widget allows you with the ability to change some design aspects of the logo of the website.

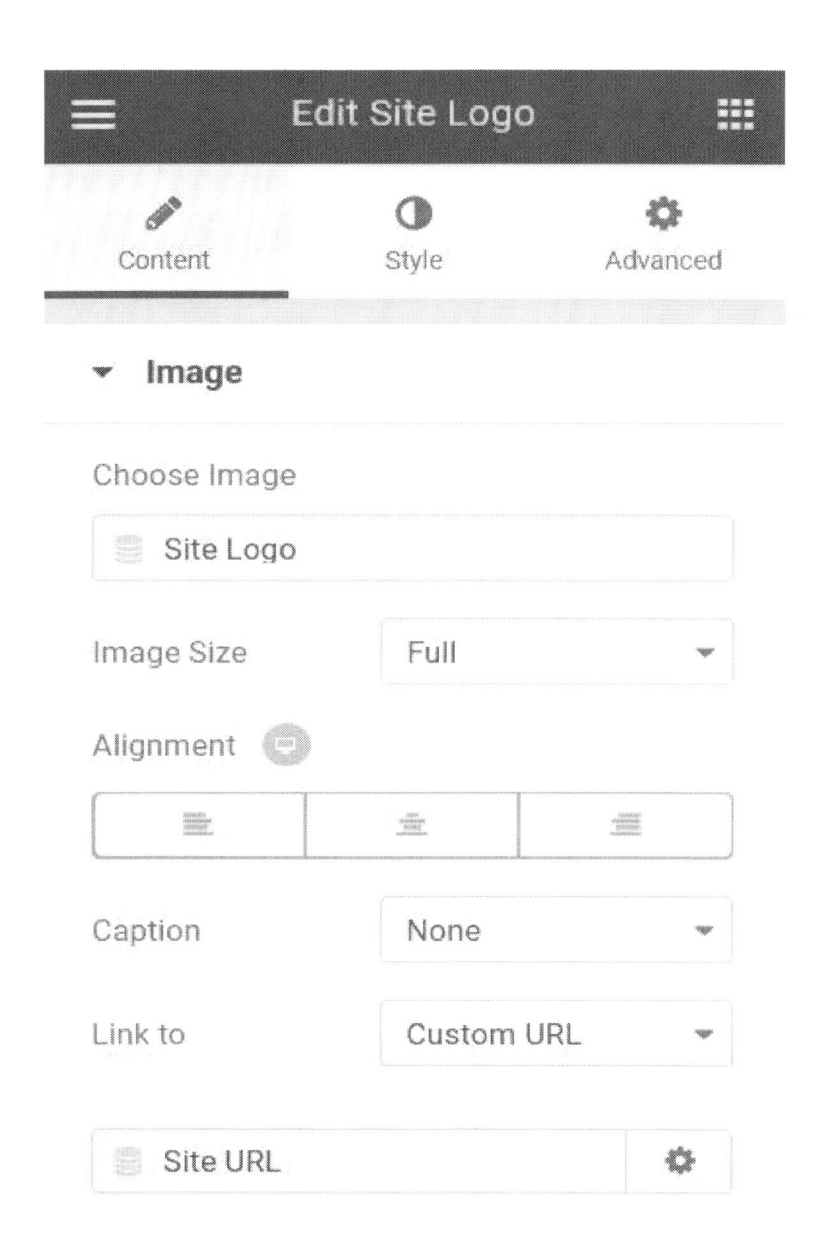

Fig 1.2: Site logo widget of elementor

The site logo widgets of elementor is made up of two main sections. These sections are "Content" and "Style". So, I will give short explanations on these two sections.

Content

The Content side has the following components:

Choose Image: The image is dynamically retrieved for you

Image Size: Set the size of the image, from thumbnail to full, or enter a custom size

Alignment: Align the site logo to the left, right, or center

Caption: Add a caption to the bottom of the image. Select from None, Attachment Caption, or Custom Caption

Link to: Set the logo's link, selecting from None, Media File or Custom Link. If Media File is chosen, set the Lightbox to Default, Yes, or No. If Custom Link is chosen, the URL will be automatically, dynamically retrieved for you.

Style

Width: Set the width of the image in either percentage (%), pixels (px), or viewport width (vw).

Max Width: Set the maximum width of the image as a percentage.

Opacity: Set the opacity level

CSS Filters: Set CSS Filters: Blur, Brightness, Contrast and Saturation

Border Type: Select the type of border, choosing from none, solid, double, dotted, dashed, or grooved

Border Radius: Set the border radius to control corner roundness

Transition Duration (only on Hover): Set the hover animation duration

Hover Animation (only on Hover): Choose an animation effect when hovering over the icon, such as Grow, Pulse, Skew, etc.

Chapter 2

WordPress, Elementor Templates and Benefits of Building a Website with Elementor

WordPress is the most used content management system. WordPress is a publishing platform that makes it easy for anyone to publish online, and proudly powers millions of websites. WordPress brought in dynamism into the world of website building. It makes it easy for people to build websites of various kinds without having ideas on how to write codes.

Unlike those days when people must have ideas on how to write codes mainly HTML and CSS, WordPress have given many people opportunity to do many things without stress. In fact, WordPress opened doors for limitless operation by users who want to build functioning websites. Users can just learn basic skills and within few times start building professional websites on their own.

Indeed, the coming of WordPress opened doors of possibilities for us.

There is difference between Wordpress.org and wordpress.com irrespective of the fact that they are all Content Management Systems.

Using WordPress comes in three flavors:

- Fully hosted with WordPress.com

-WordPress.com with an upgraded plan, like our Business Plan that allows a lot of self-hosted functionality, like plugins and custom themes and

- The self-hosted version, whose software is available for free at WordPress.org. This requires purchasing hosting with another provider, such as Bluehost, GoDaddy, etc. and installing WordPress software on it.

In this teaching I will be focussing on the third form of WordPress. This is the kind of WordPress I hosted with Inter Server website hosting company. After the hosting, I designed the WordPress site to my own taste.

The Components of WordPress Screen Options

By default, WordPress is made up of some screen options. These functions can be called the contents of WordPress as well. The components of the screen options are as follow:

- Dashboard

- Home

- Updates

- Posts

- Media

- Pages

- Comments

- Templates

- Appearance

- Plugins

- Users

- Tools

- Settings and

- Pagelayer

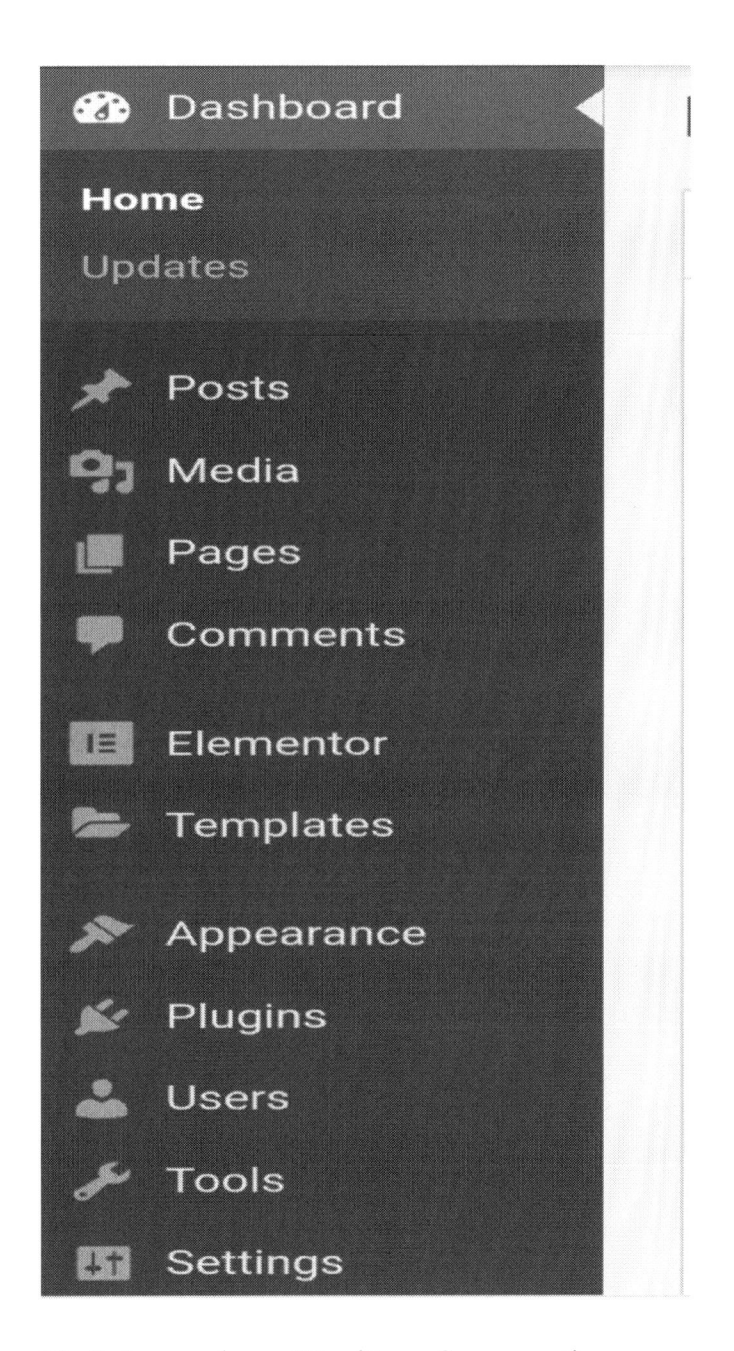

Fig 2: Image shows WordPress Screen options

From the list of the components, I omitted Elementor because it is not a default component. It appears there because I installed and activated it differently.

Dashboard

When you login to WordPress, the dashboard becomes the first place you are taken to. The admin dashboard is the first screen option on WordPress content management system.

Home

This is part of WordPress admin dashboard. When you are at the "Home" of the WordPress, you can start operating other features.

Updates

The updates screen option gives you notification of something new about your website. Maybe a plugin in WordPress is out of date, you are notified through Updates. You will see red colored attached design informing you that there is something new. Sometimes the color can be yellow depending on how important the task you are expected to carryout is.

When there is new version of WordPress or elementor available, you see that through Updates tab. It is when you click on the tab that you will be shown in detail on what the notification is all about.

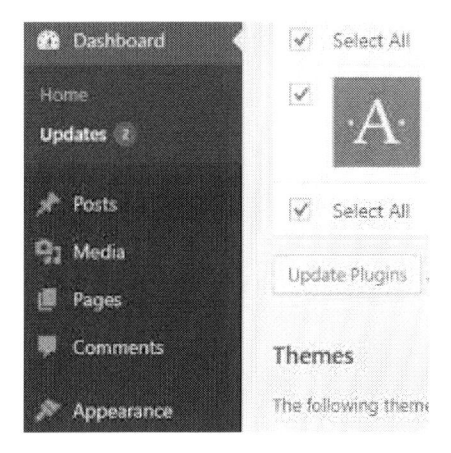

Fig 2.1: Updates tab shows notification

Always check your WordPress Updates tab because there may be something affecting your site health which you are expected to fix.

Posts

Posts section is what carries the articles on your website, allows you to publish new one and allows you to make changes to previously published ones. Posts tab is the heartbeat of many blog sites.

Media

Media on the other hand stores pictures that are available on your website. With the media tab, you can also upload some important pictures to your website. Depending on the kind of theme you are making use of, Media can store default images. From these images, you can use few to build your website if they match what your website is about.

Pages

A page is an advanced form of a post. When people visit a website, the first place they see, or land is on a page. That is usually called a landing page or a home page.

A page in WordPress usually refers to the page post type. It is one of the default pre-defined WordPress post types. In most websites, the menu tabs like Home, Contact, Services, About us and the rest are all pages. They were just added up as menu items.

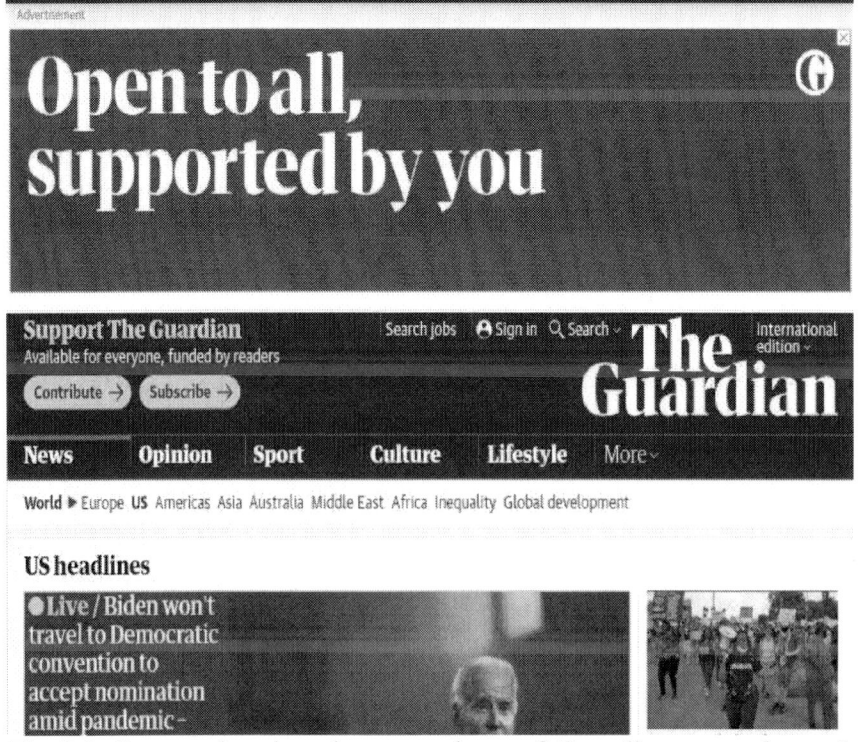

Fig 2.2: Image showing the menu bars of Guardian news formed

from page

From Fig 2.2, News, Opinion, Sport, Culture, and Lifestyle are all menu bars which were created from pages.

In WordPress, when you select Pages, you are left with two options. One is "Add New" and the other is "All Pages". The All Pages option allows you to see all the pages you have already published on your website. On the other hand, the "Add New" allows you to create new pages.

Comments

Comments screen option is gateway to all comment related function of your WordPress site. Through this tab, you can see all the comments posted by visitors to your website. You can also access the names of the people that commented under the posts on your website through this tab.

Another function you can carry out through "Comments" screen option is to set the status of every comment. Maybe a comment is abusive, and you feel may discourage readers from reading your post, you can disapprove such comment through this channel. On the other hand, you can delete certain comments through this tab. Comment screen option is the control panel to comments posted on your website.

Templates

Templates help you give your website more beautiful look. Templates works in accordance with elementor. So, it is a function that helps elementor to work well. When you select templates, you see other options. These options are "Saved Templates", "Theme Builder", "Popups", "Add New" and "Category".

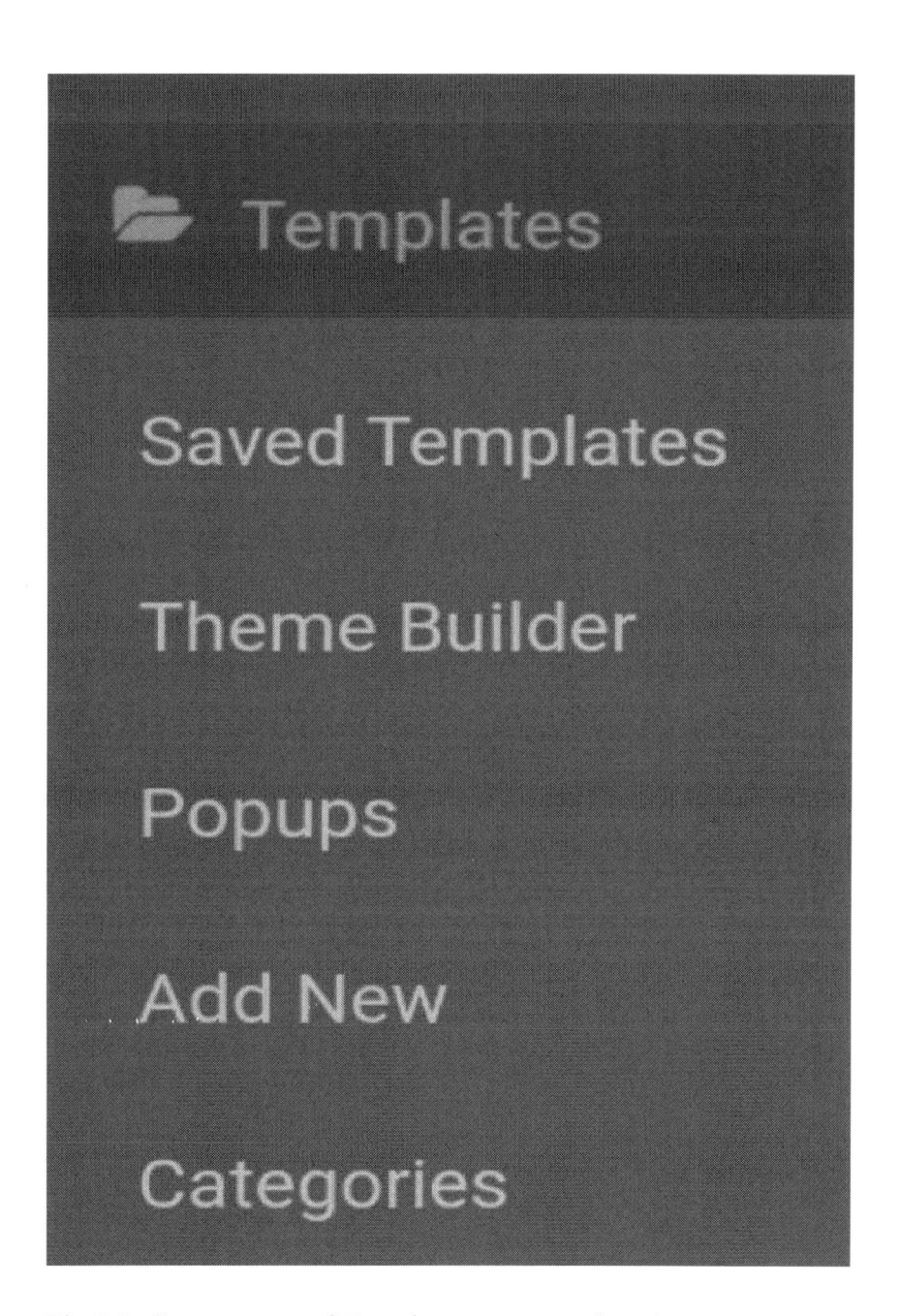

Fig 2.3: Components of Templates screen option shown

Appearance

Appearance contains many other functions. You can customize your website, change your website theme, affect your starter template, build website menus and alter the codes of your website theme through appearance. But in terms of the theme editor, do not go there if you do not have good experience in coding. Just let it be as it has been.

Plugins

Plugins are unique software that add additional functionality to WordPress websites. Plugins are created by developers and WordPress gives the developers permission to have them on their platform to allow website builders to make use of them. A plugin is a piece of software containing a group of functions that can be added to a WordPress website. They can extend functionality or add new features to your WordPress websites.

Users

Users screen option on a dashboard plays the role of keeping the number of administrators that operate the website. Sometimes in big media companies, they utilize WordPress Users properly. It allows them to add persons that can cover a different genre published on the website.

Maybe William is good at Education topics, he is created as a user to publish education articles. And if Smart is good at tech topics, he is added as a user to handle and write in that area. This makes good websites to have more contents on their websites and build more readers.

They can be in their respective areas and do their publications. This is because once they are created, they are given access to login to the site dashboard and make their publication. They are given passwords and usernames to login.

Also, sometimes editors are added. The function of the editor is to quickly edit any work written by any user. Once the editing is completed, he goes on and publish the article.

Creating users in WordPress allows you to add people with different roles, and access privileges to your site. Once created, a user will be able to log in to your site with a username and password. WordPress user roles include site administrator, editor, author, contributor and subscriber.

Editors screen option adds dynamism to WordPress sites. It is a welcomed feature added by WordPress. This has lessened the burden of having one person do all the publishing work by companies. It also encourages division of labor as certain tasks are divided among members. With this feature, everyone participates in making works done easily.

Editors have its components as "All Users", "Add New" and "Your Profile". With all users, you can see the number of users that are already existing on the website. It also shows the individual email addresses of all the users, the number of posts they have published and their profiles. You can add your profile picture through this link.

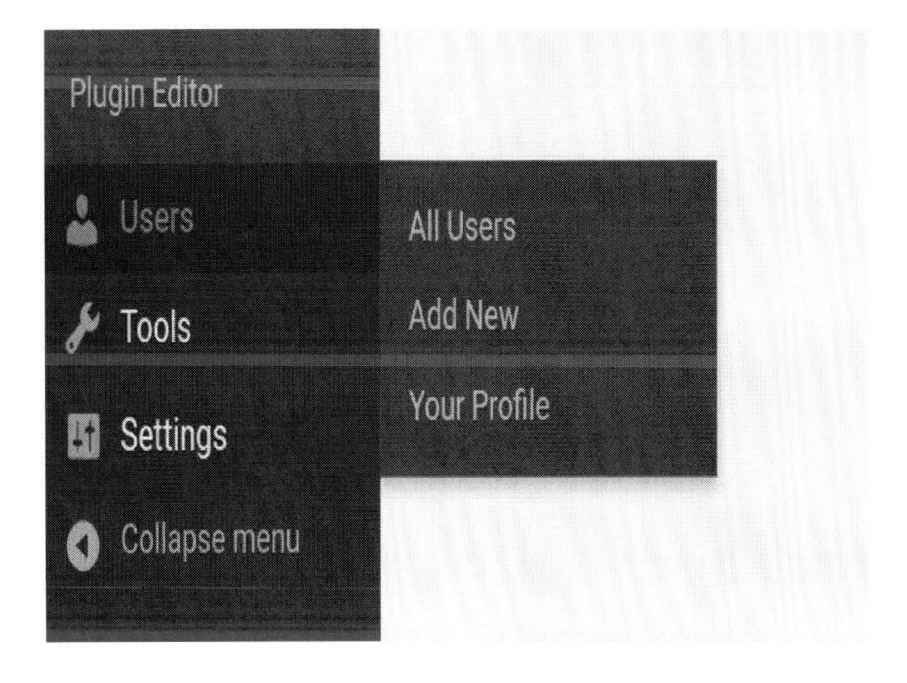

Fig :2.4: Picture showing the components of Users screen option

With Add New, you can add any person you want to welcome into the team. The person may have his already existing website but wants to work on your website as a contributor. The information to fill when you are adding a new user are Username, Email, First Name, Last Name, Website of the user if any, Password, Send

User Notification, Role. Role defines what the new user is going to be working as. As of the time of publication of this book, the roles available are Subscriber, Contributor, Author, Editor and Administrator.

In the Profile tab, it allows the user to build his profile. Through this link, a user decides on whether to have picture in his profile or not, whether he wants to change the name that appears public to readers or not and to tell people a little about his person.

Through Profile link, the user decides whether to create new password different from the one he or she uses to login to the site. It is an optional thing. But if he does not want any new password, he can continue with the one he uses to login.

Building websites with WordPress makes it easy for you to do many things as a builder. If in the long run a user decides to leave the team of users, it is possible. The administrator can remove you from the list of users.

Tools

Tools has special functionality that makes WordPress websites complete. Tools is a menu tab in the WordPress admin sidebar. It contains tools to perform some non-routine management tasks.

Tools are made up of few other components for performing specific tasks. The components are "Available Tools", "Import",

"Export", "Site Health", "Export Personal Data", and "Erase Personal Data". Each of these links is used to complete a specific task.

```
Plugins
Users
Tools
Available Tools
Import
Export
Site Health
Export Personal Data
Erase Personal Data
Settings
Collapse menu
```

Fig 2.5: Tools screen option and its components

With Available Tools, you can view some of the tools you have already installed into the system from outside the WordPress. If you have not imported any files from outside WordPress before, this link will be empty and will not show any report when you select it.

Import allows you to import files from other content management systems like Google Blogger and Live Journal. The import tool contains scripts to import data from other Content Management Systems into WordPress.

Take for example you have some nice posts you published on

Google Blogger and now you want to publish them in your newly hosted site with WordPress, this import tab can help you achieve that. Instead of doing copy and paste, Import tool makes it easy for you.

The export tool allows users to export WordPress data in XML format which can later be imported into another WordPress installation. The format is called a WordPress eXtended RSS or WXR file. It will contain all your posts, comments, custom fields, categories, and tags. Exporting your content is a useful way to back up your WordPress website.

Site Health tab tells you how healthy your website is. It shows whether your site is in a good state or in a critical condition. Honestly this is a new feature developed by WordPress and it has really helped administrators maintain the health state of their websites.

With this tool, you are informed on the plugins in your site that need to be removed or made inactive. These plugins are mainly those ones that are not in use. In the other words, they are occupying space.

Site Health tool also informs you of the themes that you are not using on your website and hence they are still active in the background of your website. Some of the themes are those you have used before but later you decided to install another theme and start using that new theme. Site Health encourages you should deactivate such themes that are no longer in use. It encourages that you should remove such inactive theme. A link is usually provided for you to do that immediately to improve the health of your website.

If your WordPress site is running outdated PHP version, Site Health tool will let you know. It can detail out reasons you need to upgrade. Also, it can give you a direct link for the upgrade.

Export Personal Data involves personal request. With the changes and focus on privacy in the internet, WordPress has taken steps to allow for users of your WordPress site to be able to request the removal of their personal data. The added interface allows for the administrator to request a confirmation for data export and removal.

Erase Personal Data is a newly added tool component by WordPress. WordPress 4.9.6 included a feature to delete a user's personal data upon verified request. Deleted data is permanently removed from the database. Erasure requests cannot be reversed after they have been confirmed.

Settings

Settings Screen option records the settings of your entire website. It shows the settings that affects you as the user and the one that affects that of your readers also. From settings, you can change any permission you do not like about your website.

The Sittings include General, Writing, Reading, Discussion, Media, Permalinks and Privacy Settings. In General, you have your website name, Website URL, description, time zone of the site, date and time format, Administrator's email, new subscribers, membership, the website language and usage tracking.

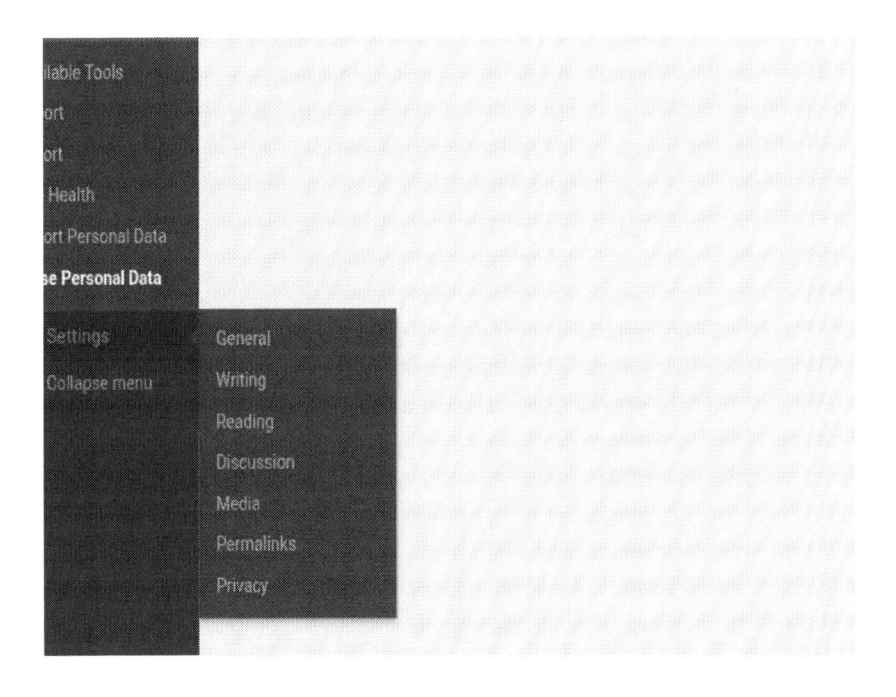

Fig 2.6: Settings screen option

The Writing shows settings on how you write while the Reading is settings concerning what people read on your website. For the Reading settings, you set the number of posts you want to appear on your landing page, whether latest posts are to show first on your landing page or not and whether search engine should discover your website or not. Example of Search engine is Google.

In the Discussion settings, you set how you want people to discuss about your posts through comments section. You set whether you have to approve some comments before they go public or not, the maximum number of comments to be shown on each post, whether readers should fill their names and email before they comment and whether avatar are to be used to show readers that comment on your posts.

In Media settings, the admin shows the dimensions and size of images to be uploaded to the site. He also instructs the system on how images and videos to be uploaded to the site are organized.

Permalinks settings is all about the links on the site. It sets how the links to posts published on the site should be modeled. For example, date and name can be used to structure the link. Example, if I am to publish a tile "Web Design" in my website www.teachkindle.com, the link to the article using the given format will be like https://teachkindle.com/2020/05/31/web-design/.

Privacy settings allows you to set privacy policy on your website. As a website owner, you may need to follow national or international privacy laws. For example, you may need to create and display a Privacy Policy.

Elementor Templates

Elementor plugin comes with many templates. These templates are but not limited to:

- Blog templates

- Portfolio templates

- E-commerce templates

- Small business templates, example coffee tea restaurant templates

- Templates for vacation websites

- Gallery templates and

- Corporate organization templates

The Benefits of Building Websites with Elementor

The benefits of building websites with elementor are as follow:

- It helps to easily create blog sites with suitable blog templates

- It makes website design easy because of its drag and drop properties

- It makes building of e-commerce websites easy

- It gives visual view of websites as you build on them

- It makes it possible to build portfolio websites within few minutes

- Elementor has many functionalities. Some features of its pro version cannot be found in other page builders

- It gives room for users to design different pages differently with unique template designs.

Chapter 3

Choosing a Domain Name and Hosting

This is the real thing in website creation. It is where the journey of creating website starts from. If you have no domain name, there is no way you will own a website and there is nowhere we can use elementor. The first thing you must do in creating an any website for yourself or someone else is to choose a domain name.

A domain name is that name which you want your website to answer. A domain name is your website name. A domain name is the address where internet users can access your website.

The first thing is to pick a domain name and another thing is to check whether the domain name is available for your proposed website to answer. Yes, that is it. If the domain name has been taken by someone else, you cannot answer that domain name. Example, for the website www.amazon.com, the domain name is "amazon". What that implies is that there cannot be two "amazon" on the web. That unique name has been given to the company by domain name registrars.

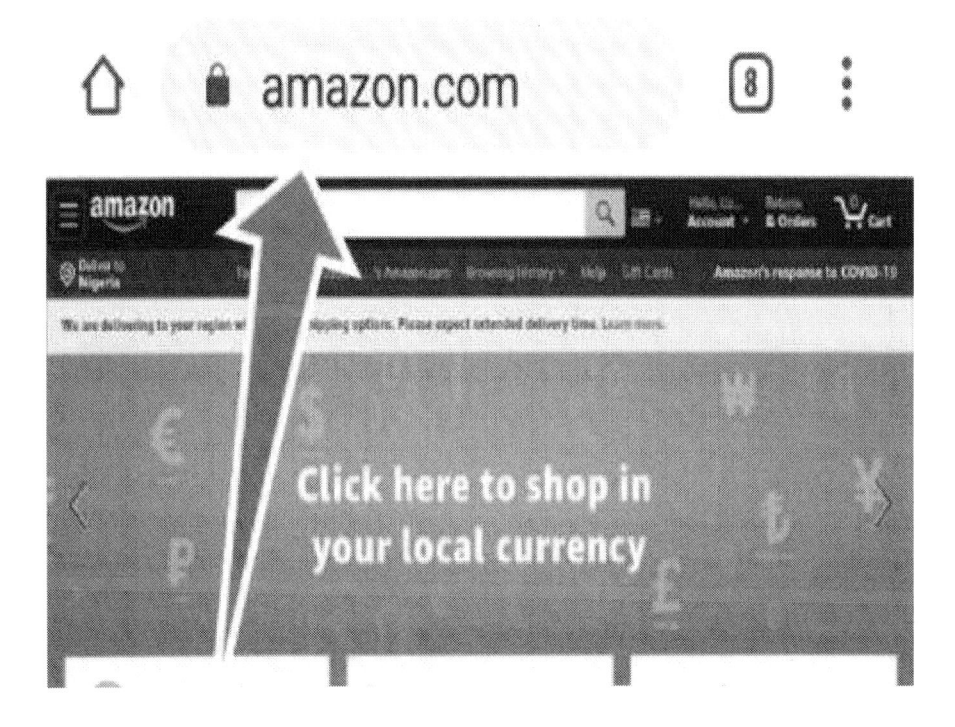

Fig 3: Picture showing amazon as a domain name

What you should know in Choosing Domain name

There are things you need to know before you choose a domain name. These are as follow:

- A domain name is combination of letters that forms a unit. What I mean is that the letters that form the domain name cannot be separated from each other. For example, you can have a domain name as "donsmart" but cannot have a domain name as "don smart". That space is not allowed.

- A domain name once chosen and registered cannot be changed. Before you register a domain name, you should know that it cannot be changed until it expires. Otherwise, you register another domain name for yourself, and that will be double expenses.

- Make your domain name short and easy to capture. It is better you make your domain name short and something that will be easy for people that visit your website to remember. If you want to make it long, just do it in a way that people can remember it. It is better to have a website URL as "www.smartlearn.com" than having "www.uzkytrarn.com".

Can you see the difference in the two? The domain name "smartlearn" can easily be remembered by buyers than "uzkytrarn". Visitors will find it difficult to pronounce that second domain name. This will make them not to visit the site if they want to visit it again later. Because they could not pronounce the name, they could not visit the site as they forgot the domain name.

Domain Name Registration

You must first register your domain name through any website hosting company. It is this hosting company that will make sure that your website is always online. In the other words, they will make sure that your files are stored in their server. Any time people visit your website, these files appear as products and posts in their eyes.

There are several website hosting companies you can host your website with. When you visit their websites, you first check with their tool on the website to know if the website name you want to take is available. If it is, you can proceed with the registration.

At the end, you pay the company and then they register your domain for you. The website hosting company on their own then take the money for domain name registration, for giving you domain name, and for keeping your files and web active on the internet.

Some hosting companies allow people to pay for at least one-year hosting of their websites. But in the recent time we have seen some changes in the duration of hosting. There are some registrars of websites that can allow you to pay for 1 to 3 months period. An example of such domain name registrar (also the same with website hosting company) is Inter Server with website URL as www.interserver.net.

Fig 3.1: Inter Server homepage

If you are a beginner, you can start with this website hosting company. Inter Server is cool and fine for people who do not know much about web building. With this company, you can just subscribe for 3 months to experiment on what you have learned and what you are going to learn. After that you can decide whether to extend it and continue making use of the site.

There are many website hosting companies today. In United States alone, there is over 900 website hosting companies in the country. It is your choice to make on the one you want to use to host your website. The prices paid varies as well. It is like you deciding on the price to sell an item to people and another seller deciding on the price to sell that same product in his own shop.

Some website hosting companies are as follow:

- GoDaddy

- Google Cloud Platform

- Amazon Web Services (AWS)

- BlueHost

- Squarespace

- Namecheap

- HostGator

- Automattic

- Wix Hosting

- Liquid Web

- DreamHost

- Weebly

- Digital Ocean

- InMotion Hosting

- Rackspace

- Peedam Hosting

- Linode

- Leaseweb

- Media Temple

- EGI Hosting

- Cogeco Peer

- Network Solutions

- SiteGround

-HostMonster

-Psychz Networks

- iPage

-A2 Hosting

- SoftLayer

- Smart Web

- Hostway

- Inter Server

So out of the above listed website hosting companies, you are to make your choice on the one to use. They are all confirmed domain name registrars. In the next heading, I will be taking you on the practical approach on how to register a domain name through any of the hosting companies.

Practical: Step-by-Step Guide in Registering your Domain Name

Step 1

Visit the website of any of the above listed website hosting companies. If you do not know the direct link or the URL of the hosting company, you can search for the name through Google. The website of BlueHost is https://www.bluehost.com, that of GoDaddy is https://uk.godaddy.com, and that of Inter Server is https://www.interserver.net.

Step 2

Check for the domain name availability. You are to search through the homepage of the hosting company you visit to know if that name you want to give your website is available. There is usually a search box provided for you to do so on the website.

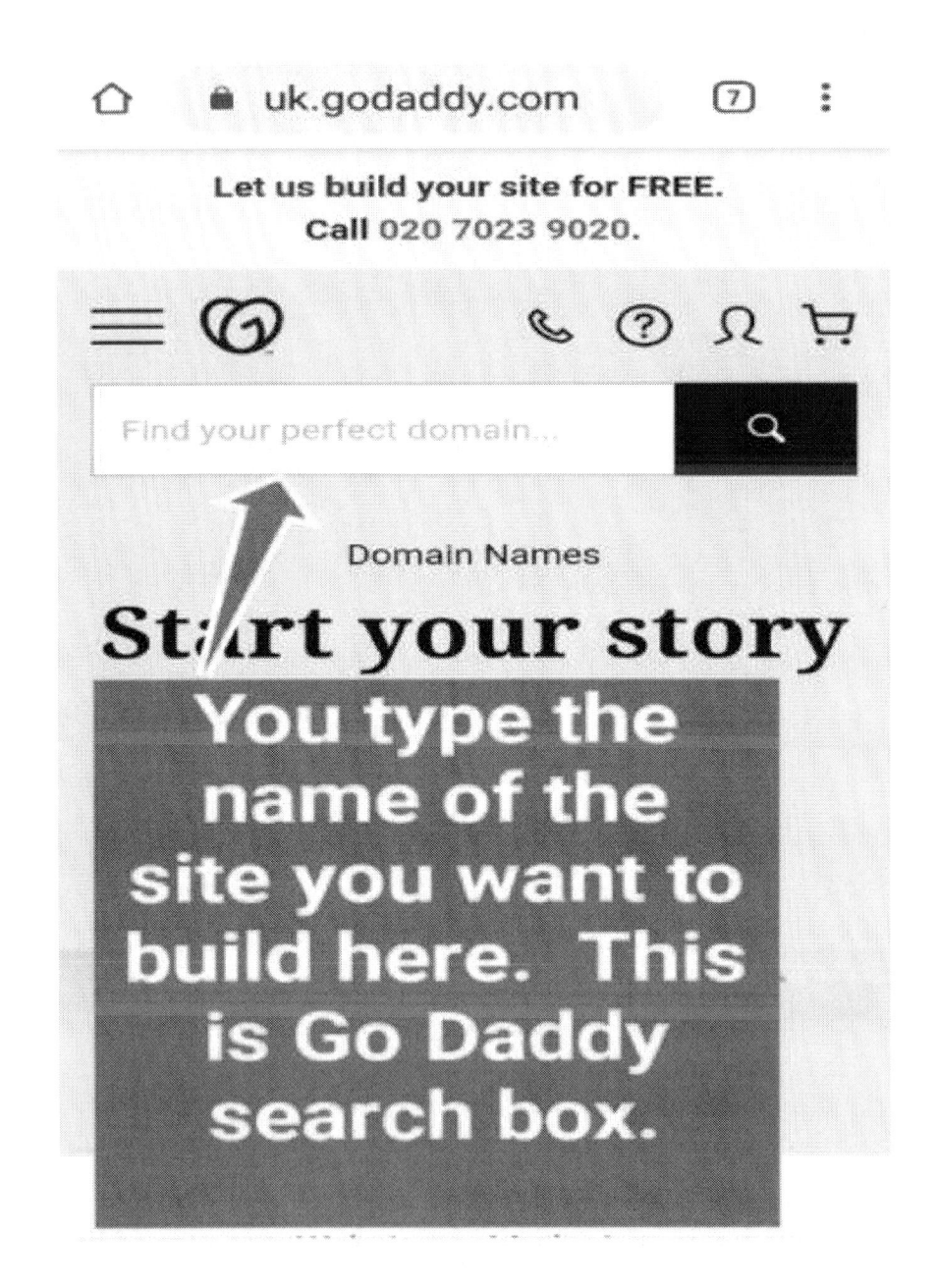

Fig 3. 2: Searching for domain name availability

If you search and the name has been taken, you have to try another name. You keep trying until you get the one that is free. But sometimes, if a domain name has been taken, the person that took it can still resell it to you if he or she has not built complete website on it. But he or she will do that at higher price if you really need it. Example is the experience I hard when I wanted to register techkindle before I finally chose teachkindle.

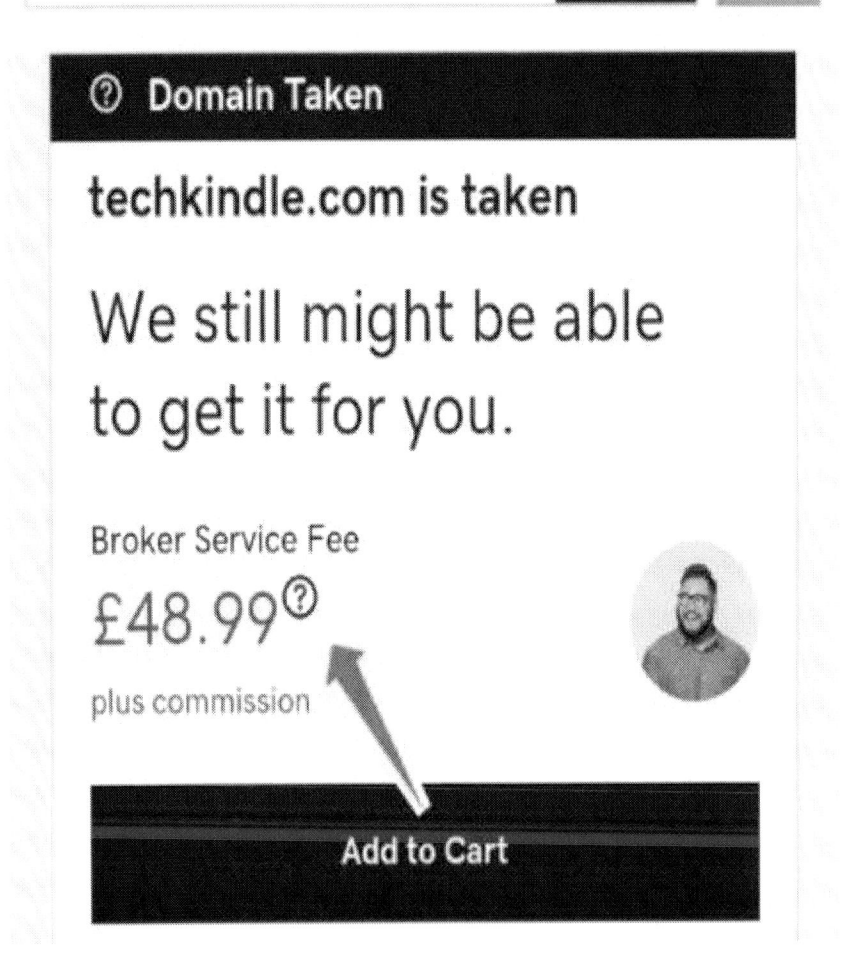

Fig 3.3: When someone has taken your domain name choice but wants you to pay higher to get it.

Step 3: Building with the Available Domain Name

Because the name I wanted to use for my website was not available and I didn't want to pay that amount of money to get it from the person that first registered it, I then try another name.

At this stage I chose to try another domain name called "teachkindle". If I tried and the name was free, I went on with it. But if it was not available, I would keep on trying. Once the domain was available, I saw a message like "CONGRATULATIONS YOUR DOMAIN IS AVAILABLE".

Step 4: Sign Up with the Hosting Company

Since the name you want your website to bear is available, you then signup with the website hosting company you want to use. In the signup, you fill in the major information required from you. If you already had account with the website hosting company, you can sign in using your email address you have with them and your password.

I will show you sample. When I hosted recently, I used Inter Server hosting company. I didn't not use GoDaddy again though I searched for domain name using their platform. You can still do the same using Inter Server website hosting company. I signed up with them before I could continue to make payment for my domain name "teachkindle".

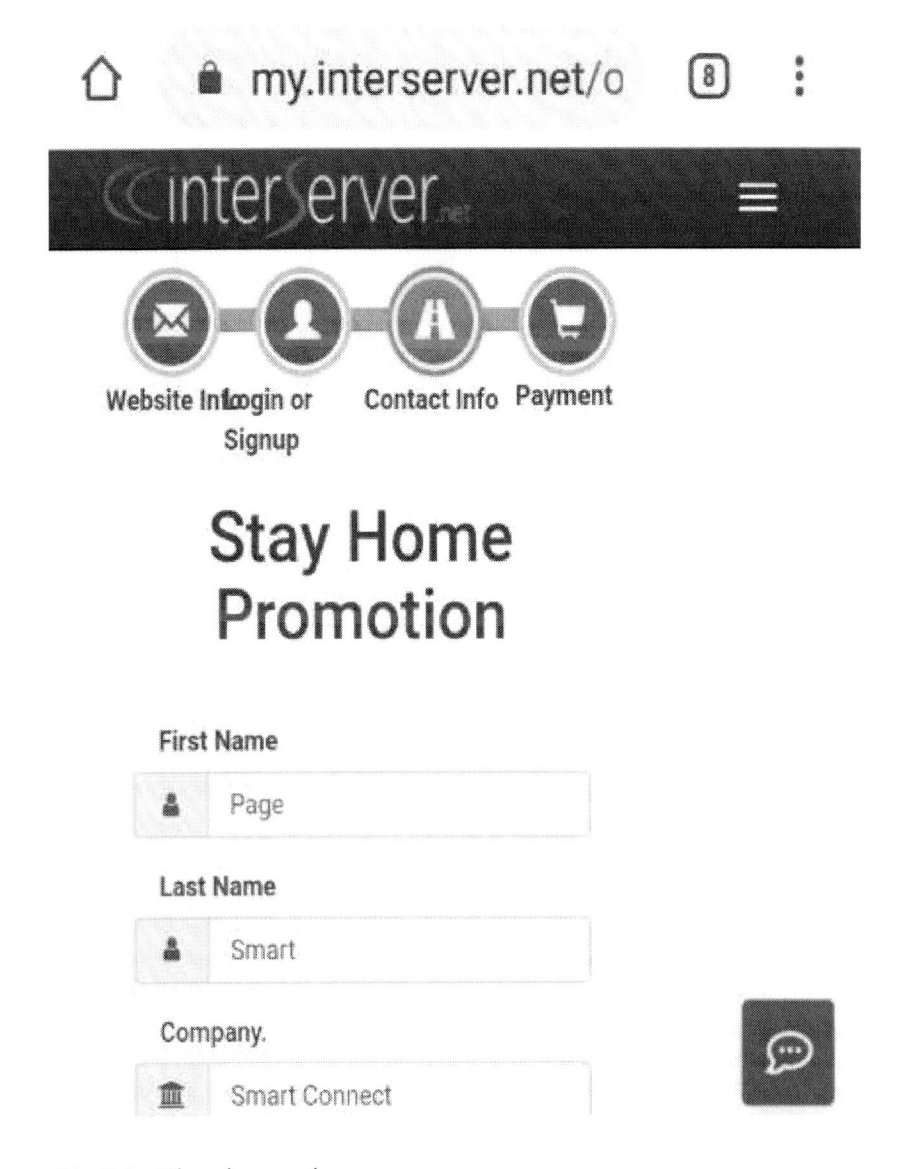

Fig 3.3: The sign up in progress

Once you sign up for an account with the company successfully, they will send you email within a short time on how to continue with your purchase of the domain name. You can get an email in this format:

"Hello!

Your InterServer account has been created.

Login Name Smart*********014@gmail.com

This sign up came from IP address **7.21*.84.**7

You can login to your account by visiting https://my.interserver.net

You can reset your password visiting https://my.interserver.net/password.php

--

Thank You,

Team Interserver"

Step 5: Login and Choose a Package

So, since you know that a particular domain you finally decided your website will answer is free, you are to login to the website of the same web hosting company. You will see "web hosting" on top or by the side of the website. Click on that and then search for the domain name again in the search box for verification purpose. The congratulations message showing you that the name is free will come up again.

You will be shown some packages. The packages vary by price. The reason is because each package has some features that make them higher than the other. In Inter Server for instance the packages the hosting company has are STANDARD WEB HOSTING, RS ONE, RS TWO, RS THREE, RS FOUR, RS FIVE, ASP.NET WEB HOSTING, WORDPRESS MANAGED HOSTING, and STAY HOME PROMOTION. As a beginner, I advise you go for Standard web hosting. Other website hosting companies have terms they use to categorize their packages also.

As you select any package, you will be shown how much you are to pay for a package per duration you want to own the domain. You can decide to own the domain for 3 months or a year.

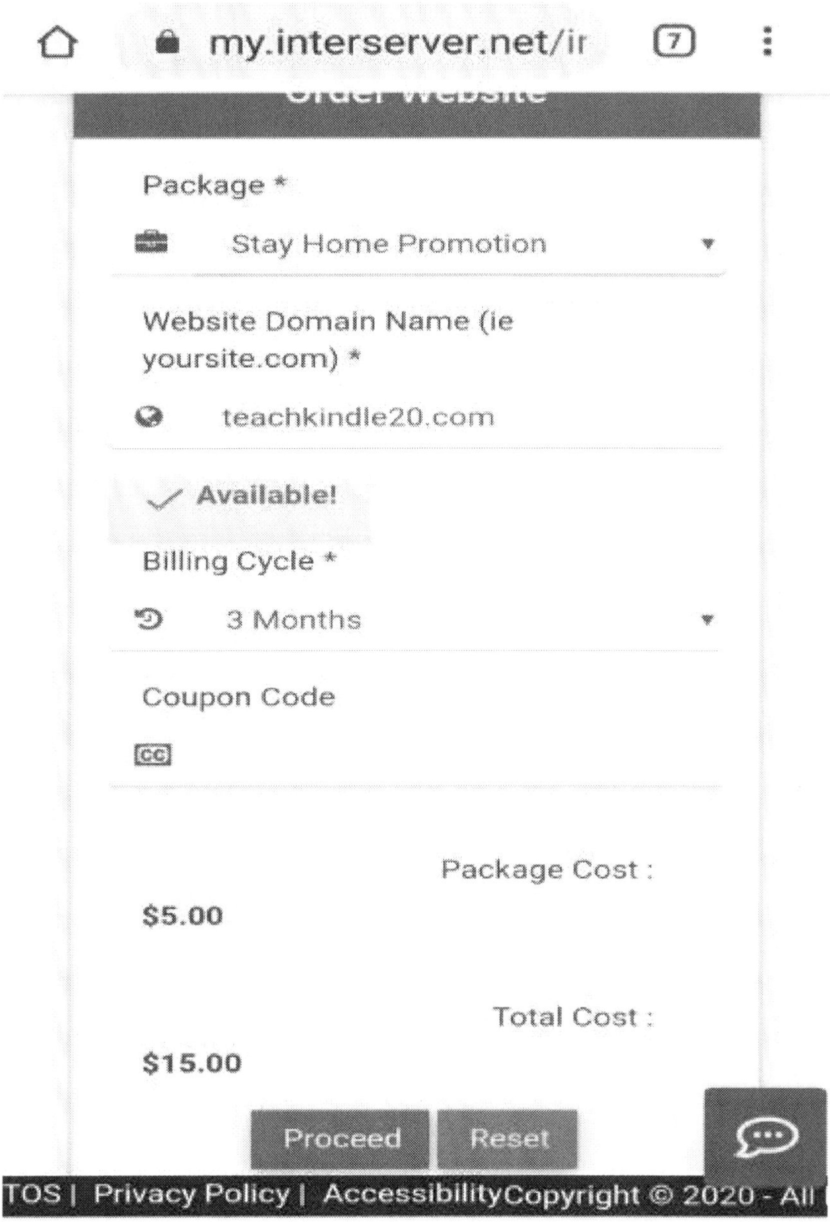
my.interserver.net/ir
7
Order Website
Package *
Stay Home Promotion
Website Domain Name (ie yoursite.com) *
teachkindle20.com
Available!
Billing Cycle *
3 Months
Coupon Code
CC
Package Cost :
$5.00
Total Cost :
$15.00
Proceed
Reset
TOS | Privacy Policy | AccessibilityCopyright © 2020 - All

Fig 3.4: Picture showing standard package chosen for a domain and the amount to pay

Note: The domain name teachkindle20.com was chosen for this particular demonstration. In other stages and this entire teaching, we will be using **teachkindle.com** for most of our illustrations.

Step 6: Billing and Payment

This is the next step. Then when you proceed to the next step after choosing your plan, you will be shown an invoice of how much you will pay.

You will be given some options on the method you want to use to make the payment. Some hosting companies has up to 3 payment options while others do have less. You can be given the options to pay with card, direct deposit to the bank, or pay with PayPal. But some domain name registers have the option of pay with card and Payment with PayPal account.

In pay with card option, you input your debit or credit card number and the CVV number at the back of the card. CVV mean Card Verification Value. It is usually a 3-digit number at the back of credit or debit card.

Fig 3.5: Image showing the CVV of a Master Card

After you enter the information for your account to be debited, you will get a security code sent to you by your bank through your phone number asking for your approval for your account to be debited. A box will be provided for you by the hosting company to enter the code. Once you enter the code correctly in the box, your account will be debited.

You will get a confirmation email in your inbox confirming your payment. The hosting company will also send you details on how to login to your control panel and install any program/application to start building your own website. The details to be sent to you for you to be able to log in to your email is your username or email and password. You are to keep them safe.

InterServer

Payment Approved

Dear Page Smart,

Your payment of $6.99 was approved and successfully applied to your balance for your Domains.

Invoice ID	4493201
Invoice Description	(Repeat Invoice: 18744140) Whois Privacy for Domains 425304
Invoice Date	2020-05-19 13:53:26
Invoice Amount	5.00
Domains ID	425304
Domain Hostname	teachkindle.com
Domains Type	10039

Invoice ID	4493200
Invoice Description	(Repeat Invoice: 18744139) .com Domain Name Registration
Invoice Date	2020-05-19 13:53:26
Invoice Amount	1.99
Domains ID	425304
Domain Hostname	teachkindle.com
Domains Type	10039

Please let us know if you have any comments or suggestions on how to improve our service by emailing support@interserver.net.

Thank You,
InterServer Team.

Fig 3.6: Confirmation email received after paying for hosting a domain

The caption is a confirmation message I received from a website hosting company after paying for my package using credit card.

Note: Your payment may not go through after you put in the card details required from you to make payment for your domain name and hosting. You can get an error message. The error message can be because your card has not been verified. The message can be in this format:

Error! CC Disabled! Payment type credit card is currently unavailable. Remove the credit card(s) you have on file and add them again. If you continue having issues please contact us.

Error! CC Disabled! Payment type credit card is currently unavailable. Remove the credit card(s) you have on file and add them again. If you continue having issues please contact us.

Make Credit Card Payment

Invoice Description	Invoice Amount
(Repeat Invoice: 18744140) Whois Privacy for Domains 425304	$5.00
(Repeat Invoice: 18744139) .com Domain Name Registration	$1.99
(Repeat Invoice: 18744138) Stay Home	

Fig 3.7: Error message after trying to pay for my domain hosting using card

To resolve the issue, the best thing is to write to their customer care. You will be responded to within 24 hours, but it depends on the hosting company. The customer care representative will guide you on what to do to resolve this. After this and you make another attempt to make your payment, it will go through without stress. If any error massage appears again, still write to them.

Conclusion

In this chapter, I was able to guide you through on step-by-step approach on how to host your website or domain. By host, I mean how to pay for a name you want your website to answer. Also, I taught you about some website hosting companies that can help you with the hosting. So, you are to choose from the many listed. Building a website is a simple thing. If you have any question or clarification you want from me, do not hesitate to write to me. My email address is at the last page or one of the last pages of this book.

Chapter 4

Installing WordPress and Account Setup through Control Panel

Let me throw a little light on what WordPress is before going deep on how to install it. It will help you understand better what the content management system is. It will also give you knowledge on the similarity it has with other software you might have used in your computer or mobile phones before now.

WordPress (WordPress.org) is a free and open-source content management system (CMS) written in PHP and paired with a MySQL or MariaDB database. Features include a plugin architecture and a template system, referred to within WordPress as Themes.

Historically, the CMS was originally created as a blog-publishing system but has evolved to support other types of web content including more traditional mailing lists and forums, media galleries, membership sites, learning management systems (LMS) and online stores. In terms of online stores, WordPress fits in properly in this so far you use the right theme. You need understanding on WordPress before going into elementor page builder. In fact, WordPress is the gateway to elementor.

Fig 4: WordPress.org logo

In terms of number, WordPress is used by more than 60 million websites, including 33.6% of the top 10 million websites as of April 2019. It is one of the most popular content management systems used by website builders all over the world.

WordPress is easy to use, and it has good flexibility. Not only that, WordPress has many responsive themes in their system. You have thousands to choose from. It is your choice to select any from the many themes and start building your site from there.

A Step-by-step Guide on how to Install WordPress and Continue with Building of your Website

Step 1: Login to your Control Panel

After you have finished with your payment to the domain hosting company and your payment confirmed and approved, you will be sent a mail to the email address you filled with the domain hosting company. The email will contain the details you need to login to the control panel of your domain. Example of the mail can be seen below:

"ACCOUNT INFORMATION:

=====================

Plan: Stay Home Promotion

Domain: teachkindle.com

IP Address: ***.72.**5.67

CPANEL LOGIN INFORMATION:

==================

https://webhosting34004.is.cc:9883

Username: teacgain

Password: ****b80*

FTP INFORMATION:

=================

FTP (SSL/TLS available):

***.72.**5.67

Username: teachkin

Password: ***L*7**"

You must first click on the link in that detail. Using the sample, I gave, you are to click on the link https://webhosting34004.is.cc:9883. The link will take you to a page requesting you enter the username given to you and the password also. Once you do that, you will be logged in to the control panel.

Do not worry too much about what control panel is. A control panel is the administration portion of your webhosting account. It is an interface that you access to administer all the aspects of your account. Control panel of a web is like that control panel in your laptop. It is the place where things can be changed and structured.

Don't be disturbed even if you do not understand the short description properly. What should be more important to you should be how to build a working e-commerce website at the end of this teaching.

With the given information, you can them login to your control panel.

≡ cPanel

Find functions quickly by typing here.

FILES

File Manager

Images

Directory Privacy

Disk Usage

Web Disk

FTP Accounts

FTP Connections

Backup

Fig 4.1 What appears as you login to your domain control panel.

Step 2: Install WordPress

After you have login to the Control panel using the details given to you by the website hosting company, scroll down to the section named "SOFTACULOUS APPS INSTALLER". In that section, click on the WordPress symbol.

Fig 4.2: WordPress Application in control panel

When you click on "WordPress" and the application opens, scroll down and click on "Install now". And once you do this a new page opens which requires you to fill some information.

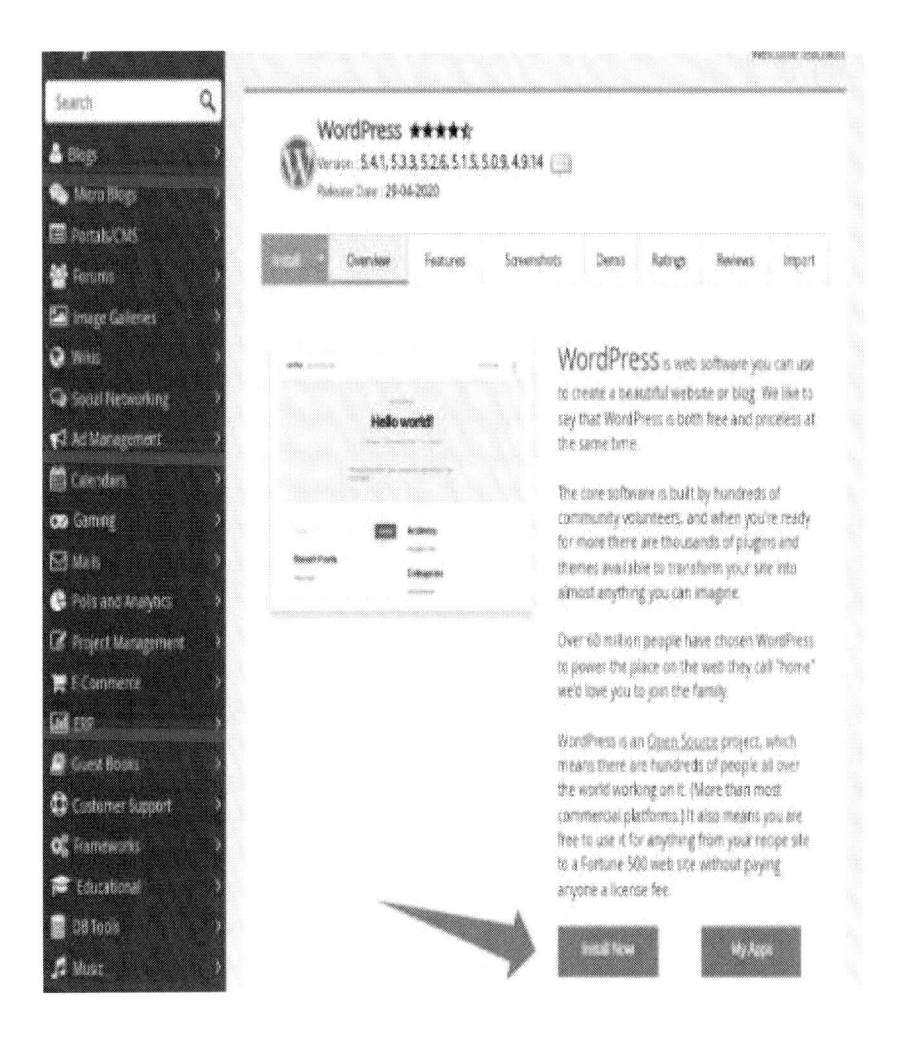

Fig 4.3: Click on the Install Now

Then fill the necessary details required from you. You must not fill in all the space, but the important boxes required of you to fill.

I want to make something clear to you, in the space of "In directory" do not fill anything there. You can still read the previous sentence again. Clear that space for everything to be empty (do not allow any letter to be there). The reason for doing this is so that you install the website in the root directory of WordPress.

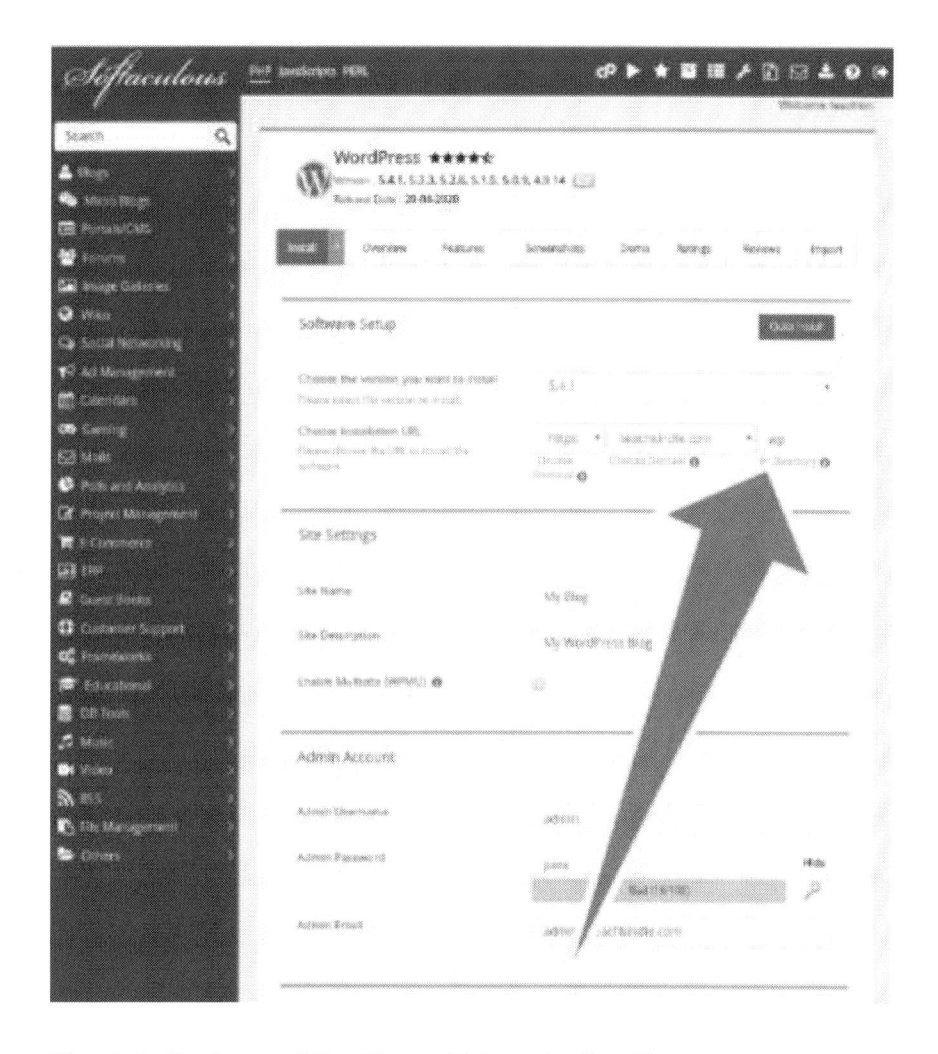

Fig: 4.4: Setting up WordPress (delete the "wp")

Using the image, you are to delete the "wp" and then leave the box empty.

Fill in the right information in the other boxes provided for you:

Site Settings Section

In the "Site Name" fill the name you want your website to answer. Using my own domain name which we have been using in this teaching, I can decide to fill my own "Site Name" as "Tech Kindle" or "Teach Kindle". The name to give the website is my choice.

But you can decide to change this name anytime you feel like doing so. That is the flexibility in building website. The only thing you cannot change is that website link (URL) which website hosting company gave you at hosting. For example, I cannot change my website (domain name) link www.teachkindle.com. It is permanent. It has been registered on the web worldwide.

In the "Site Description" you are required to describe your website shortly. So, delete that "My WordPress Blog" already put in the space by default and put few words that will tell people what your website is all about. Using my own website "teachkindle.com" I can input "TK Store" or "TEACH KINDLE". This is because I am going to build the site as an online store. When I have this in my description, it will send signal to visitors on what my website is all about whenever they visit.

For " Enable Multisite (WPMU)" do not tick the box. You are to leave it as it is.

Admin Account

In this section, you are required to fill in the name you will be known with on the website or as you login to your WordPress account after the final setup, password to be used to login to your WordPress, and email address to be used to receive email news and notifications from them (WordPress).

In the "Admin Username" you can type in your real name. You can also type in any name you like to answer.

I believe you have visited any website whereby you were shown the publisher's name on top of the page. The reason why that name shows as that is because that name was chosen as the admin name on a website run by a single person. In my own case, I can choose to put "William S. Page" as my "Admin Username".

In the " Admin Password " you are to fill in the password you will use to login into your site after setup. The password should be strong and should not be easily predicted by people. Please do not use your date of birth as your password. Also do not use your mobile phone number either.

Use a password that cannot be easily broken by hackers. You can write it down and put in a place you know people will not see it. Even if you forget your password tomorrow, you can reset it and a link to do that will be sent to your working email address.

For the "Admin Email" please do not use the email address already generated by WordPress system there. Do not make that mistake. In the image, you can see "admin@teachkindle.com" in that space filled in already. That was autogenerated. So, I will not use it. I didn't create any email like that.

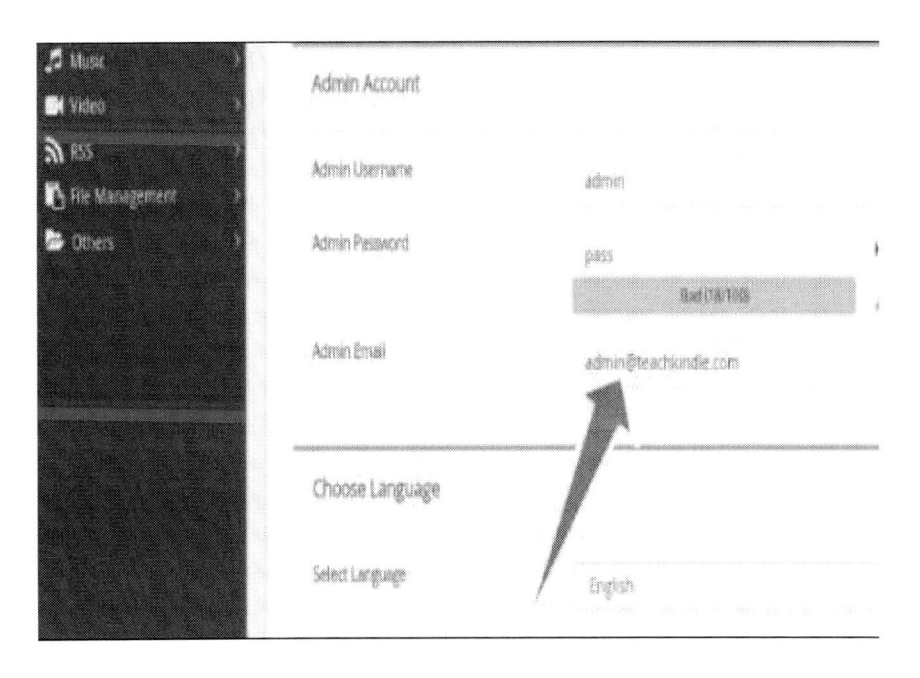

Fig 4.5: The autogenerated email address

Edit that email generated by the system and put your active email address. You can put your Gmail, Yahoomail, Hotmail, or any other email you make use of. It must not be a custom email. WordPress need that email to notify you of any changes or important news you need to know about their products. The admin section should not be played with as that can be used to help you recover your account if issues arise.

In the choose language section, just choose the language you want your website to be written in. There are many language options on WordPress. As of May 2020, there were 37 language options available in WordPress. Among these languages is English, Spanish, Chinese, German, Italian, Dutch, Greek, Hebrew, Arabic, Danish, Finnish, French, Croatian, Portuguese, Hungarian language and others.

Manage Plugin Sets

For this section, do not tamper with anything there. Just leave it as it is by default. When we are done with the installation of the WordPress, we can manage plugins from our dashboard. So, do not tick anything on "login Limit Attempts (Loginizer)", "Classic Editor" and "wpCentral - Manage Multiple WordPres".

Advanced Options

In the "Advanced Options" section, do not change anything there. Leave those options the way they are. With time when you master website building properly, you can make changes you want.

Stage 3: Theme Selection

There are many themes you can select in WordPress before you finally complete your installation. It is your choice to choose from the Plenty available themes. Themes give your website the beauty it is required to have.

In the "Select Theme" section, you are expected to make your selection. If the one you want to use does not appear first, click on the arrow pointing towards the right to see other themes. Keep on going until you see the theme you feel will fit the website you want to build. But if you do not see any which you have in mind, do not worry because you will be exposed to more themes in WordPress admin area after installation.

Fig 4.6: Arrow shows where to click when your choice of theme does not appear first

Also, if you already have the name of a WordPress theme you want to use, you can use the theme search box to search. Just put the name of the theme and hit search. The theme will pop up and you select it.

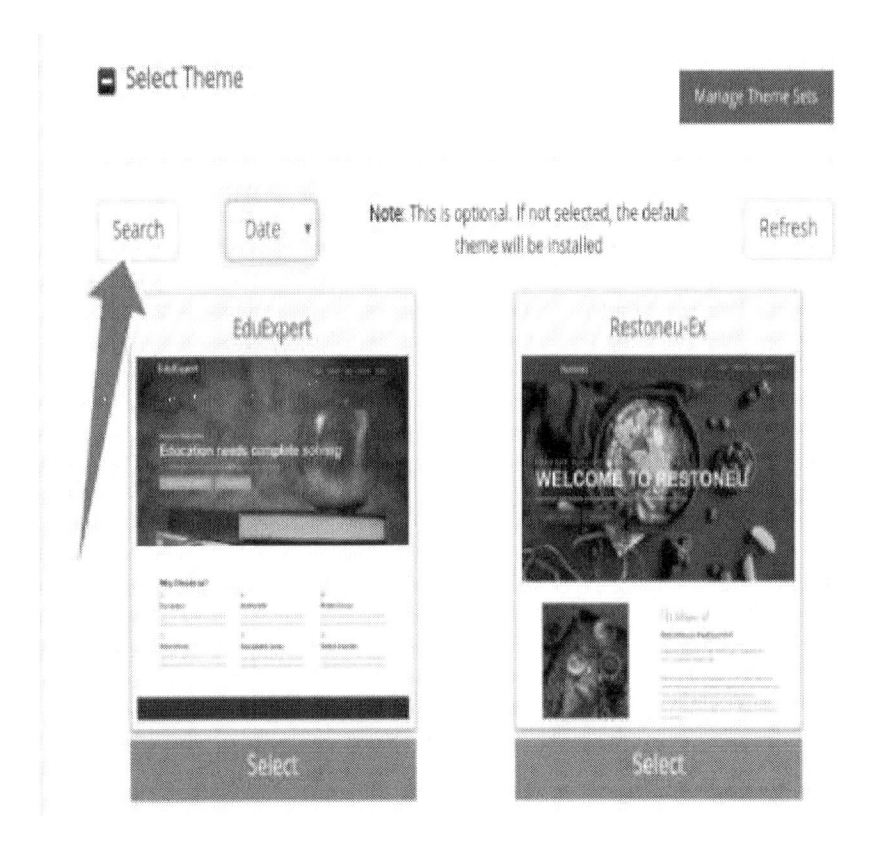

Fig 4.7: When you click on the search, a window will pop up and you type the name of the theme

Check through all the information you filled in the WordPress installation page. If you will forget your password or the email address you used in your WordPress, you can write them down or save them in any cloud application you make use of.

When you are sure that everything you filled is in order, there is something more you need to do before you hit install. At the bottom of the page, look very well and you will see "Email Installation Details to". In that box, fill in your email address you want WordPress to send your installation details to.

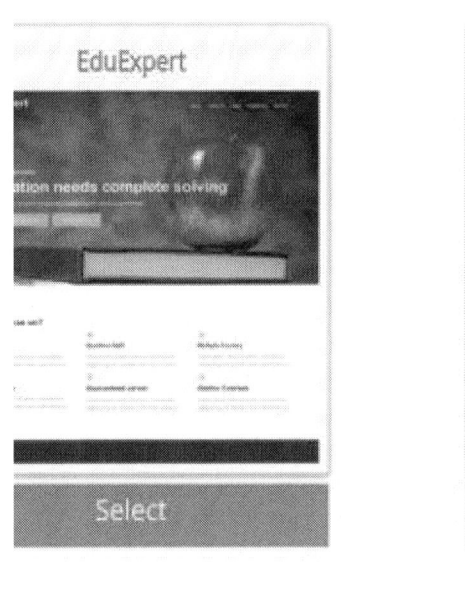

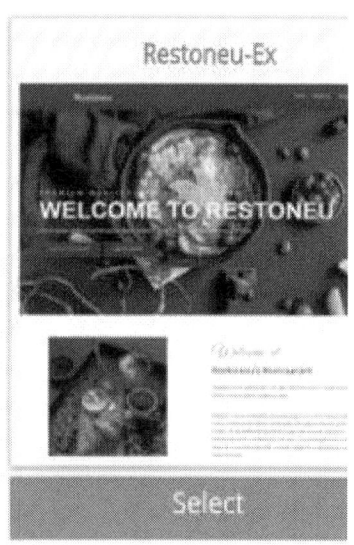

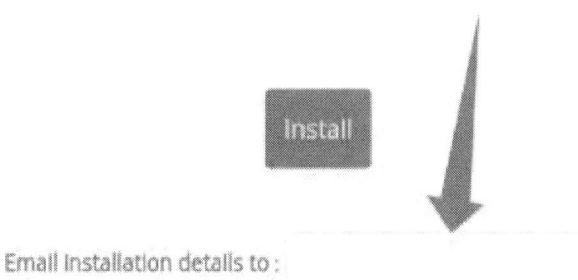

Fig 4.8: Type in your functioning email address there

When I built my first website, I forgot to fill that space. I waited for long expecting WordPress to send any installation details to my email address, but it didn't come. I later uninstalled the WordPress and reinstalled a new one filling everything correctly, that was when I got the details from them.

Installation details contains some information. The information is:

- Your website Path

- Your website URL

- Admin URL

- Admin Username

- Admin Password

- Admin Email

- MySQL Database

- MySQL DB User

- MySQL DB Host

- MySQL DB Password

- Update Notification: Enabled or Disabled

- Auto Upgrade: Enabled or Disabled

- Automated Backups: Enabled or Disabled

- Time of Installation

When you have verified every information you have entered and then select Install, the page loads and the installation is completed. Below is the similar page you will see:

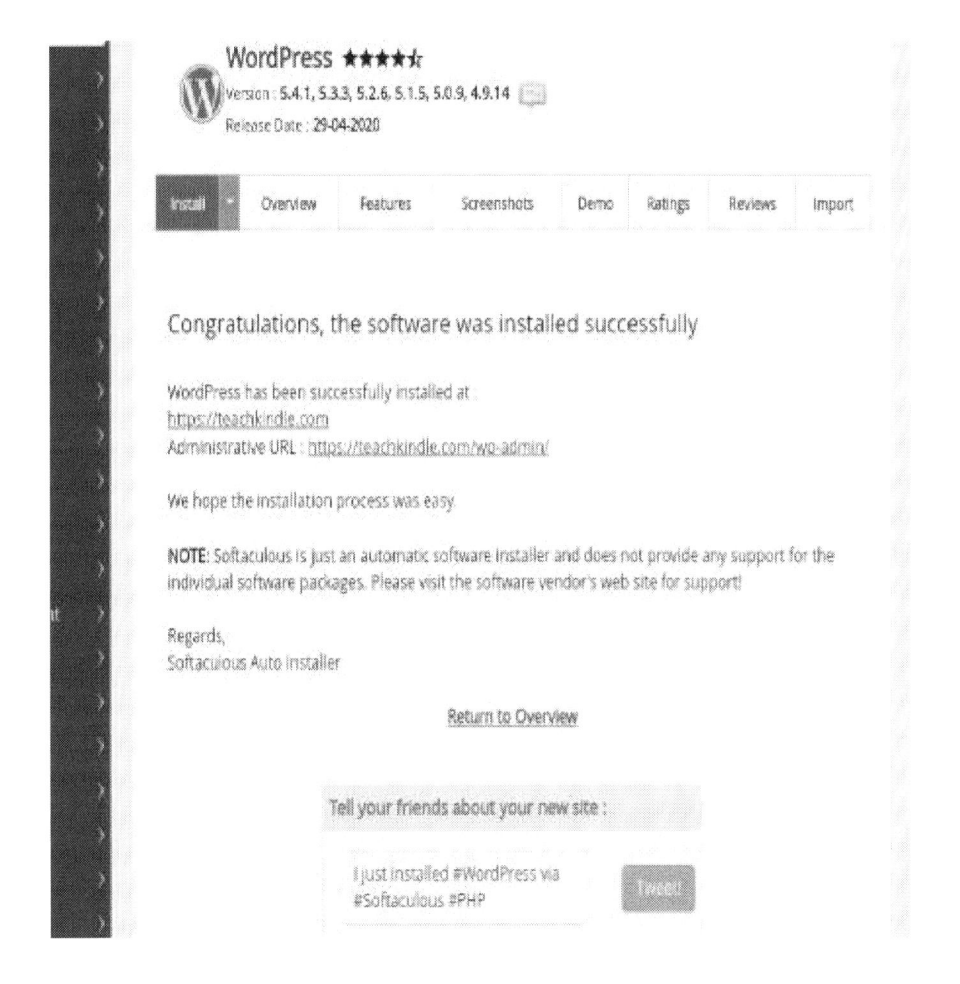

Fig 4.9: Picture shows next page that appears after installation

I used the word "similar" because my domain name is different from the one you will be using. As my own domain name is different and unique, that is why my administrative URL is unique.

You may ask what URL is? URL stands for Uniform Resource Locator. It is just a website link. In this sample, my administrative URL is https://teachkindle.com/wp-admin/. Once I type that in any browser, I can input my username and password, and login to my WordPress admin area.

So, for your own, once you installed WordPress after you have filled the necessary information required of you, your own admin URL will be https://your domain name/wp-admin/. Let us say your domain name is "uniquefood" your admin URL will be https://uniquefood.com/wp-admin/.

What will You do if after Installation your Website does not Load?

It is expected that once you put your email address where your installation details are to be sent and then hit "Install" and the installation is successful, your website suppose to start working immediately. If you visit "www.mywebsite.com" at that point, it supposes to load and open a new page.

If I visit my website www.teachkindle.com immediately after the installation is completed, it supposes to load just as I have in the picture:

Fig 4.1.1: Homepage of my newly created website

What to do when your Newly Created Website does not Load

If after the WordPress installation and your website does not load or you receive error message, there is something you can do. Without wasting much time, visit the website of the domain hosting company where you hosted your website.

Login in, and then write to them concerning the issue. They will respond to you within minutes on what caused the issue. At the end it will be resolved. Sometimes such issue occurs because the site has not been verified.

When I hosted my site teachkindle.com with Inter Server and installed WordPress for the site building, I got an error message when I visited that my website. I refreshed the page many times and the error message kept coming.

I then logged in to my account with Inter Server website and sent mail to them. They responded to me within few minutes explaining the cause of the error. I was instructed to verify my new domain that it is a rule from ICANN before my website would work. I did that and my website started loading fine.

Below is the message I got from my hosting company (Inter Server) on the issue:

"** Please note that failure to complete the process outlined below will lead to the suspension of your domain name. **

Dear Customer,

Please read this important e-mail carefully.

Recently you registered, transferred or modified the contact information for one or more of your domain name(s). ICANN requires all accredited registrars to verify your new contact information. You can read about ICANN's new policy at: http://www.icann.org/en/resources/registrars/raa/approved-with-specs-27jun13-en.htm#whois-accuracy.

teachkindle.com

In order to ensure your domain name remain active, you must now click the following link and follow the instructions provided:

http://approve.domainadmin.com/registrant/?verification_id=1089

2562&key=eUnUzdWKRy&rid=2833

Failure to follow the above link and complete this process will eventually lead to the suspension of your domain name(s).

If you have additional questions, please do not hesitate to get in touch.

Thank you for your attention,

InterServer Inc"

Chapter 5

New Theme Installation

The kind of theme you use on your website has a way of affecting its look. I took you on step-by-step guide on how to host a website with any hosting company of your choice and on how to set up WordPress Content Management System. Those teachings were well detailed out for your proper comprehension and I believe you understood them.

Please do not hesitate to write to me through my email which is at the end of this book if you have any challenge. I am here to help you build and design your own website with the application of elementor page builder in some areas. I feel happy to teach people on what they do not know because skills are very important for human's growth and development.

In one of the past chapters, I explained the features of WordPress dashboard to you. That was not a pure practical class. I did that because I want you to know the functions of each screen option. I also want you to be properly equipped and get use to those tabs.

In this chapter, we will be entering a pure practical section. I will be teaching you on sound dynamic theme you have to use to build your website easily and give it stunning design. So many things have changed in the world of website building and design over the years, and I put those changes into consideration before giving you this teaching. You will learn something great from this chapter and it will bring enlightenment to your desire to design websites.

Installation of New Theme

After you are done with setting up and installation of your WordPress through your control panel as we discussed previously, the next is to login into your WordPress admin area. As earlier said, you will be given a login URL (example https://teachkindle.com/wp-admin/) and when you enter the link in a browser, you are to insert your username or your email address and the password you used when setting up WordPress through your control panel, then hit login.

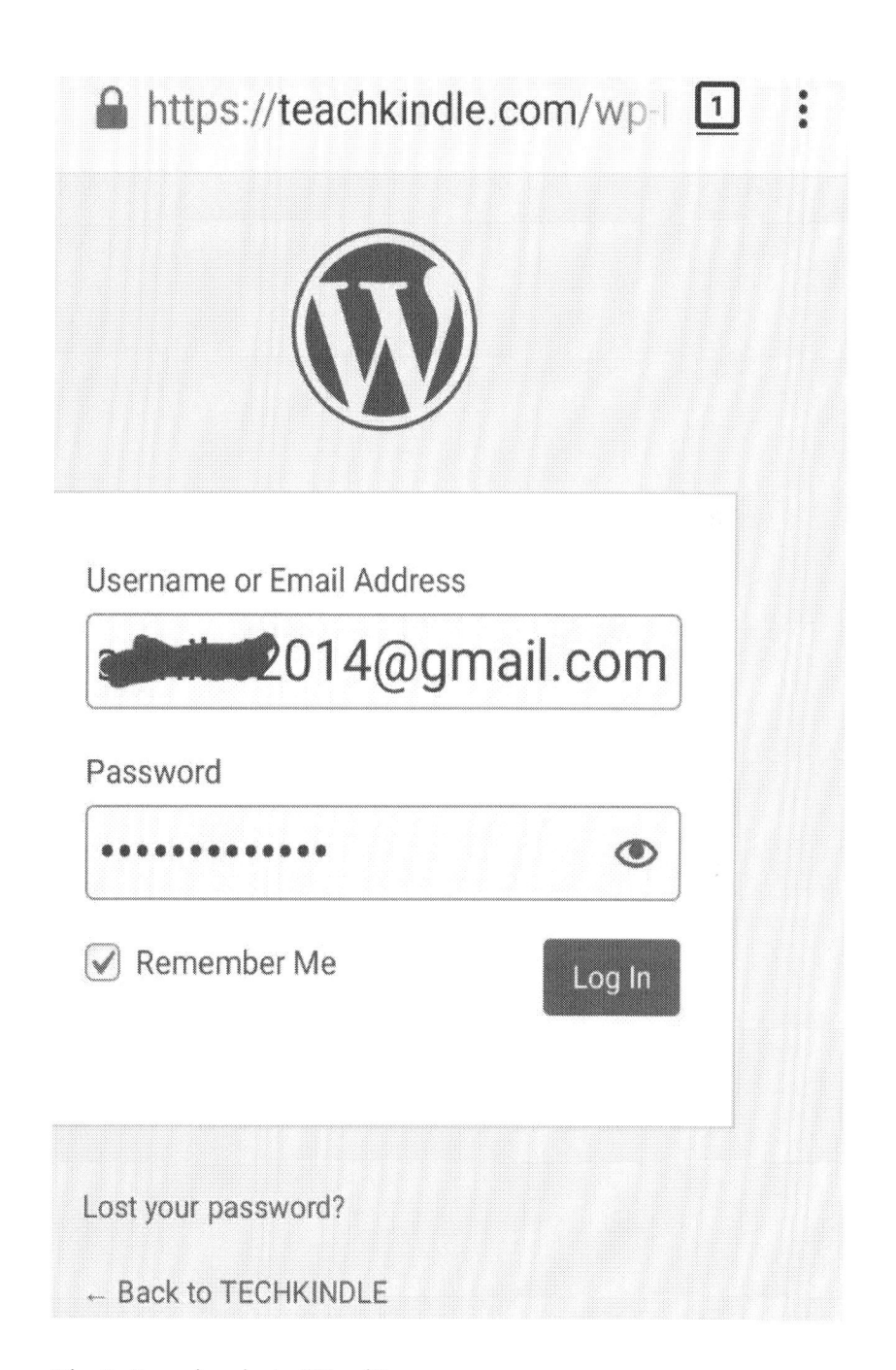

Fig 5: Logging in to WordPress

When you are done logging in to your WordPress site, the next thing you will see is your dashboard. It displays many screen options/tabs for specific functions.

You are to then install a new theme that will help us build a complete website of good standard. In this teaching, we will start by using a theme "Astra" to build our website Astra theme works well with elementor. So, prepare your mind to install and activate it. It is one of the most popular themes used by Website builders to build their websites in the recent time. You can decide to choose your own theme, but I will be teaching you with Astra.

Installation of Astra Theme

Step 1: Search and Install the Theme

As you login to your WordPress, you will be taken to the dashboard homepage. At the right-hand side, you will see some screen options. Scroll down and select **Appearance**. As you select **Appearance,** it will display some other options. So, select **Themes** among those optionally.

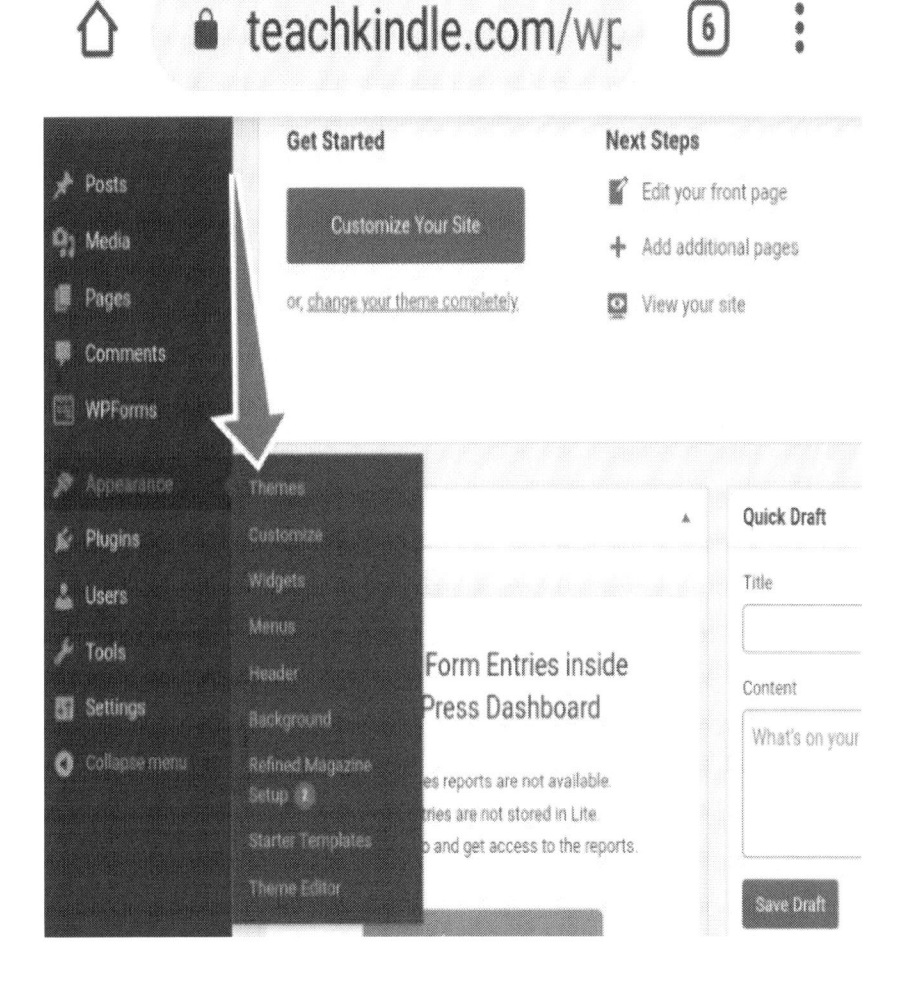

Fig 5.1: Choosing Theme option for new theme installation

As you select the Themes sub screen option, a new page will open. On top of the page you will see "**Add New**". Click on the **Add new** and a search box will be shown to you. Also, you will be shown many available themes in WordPress. In the search box, just type the word "**Astra**".

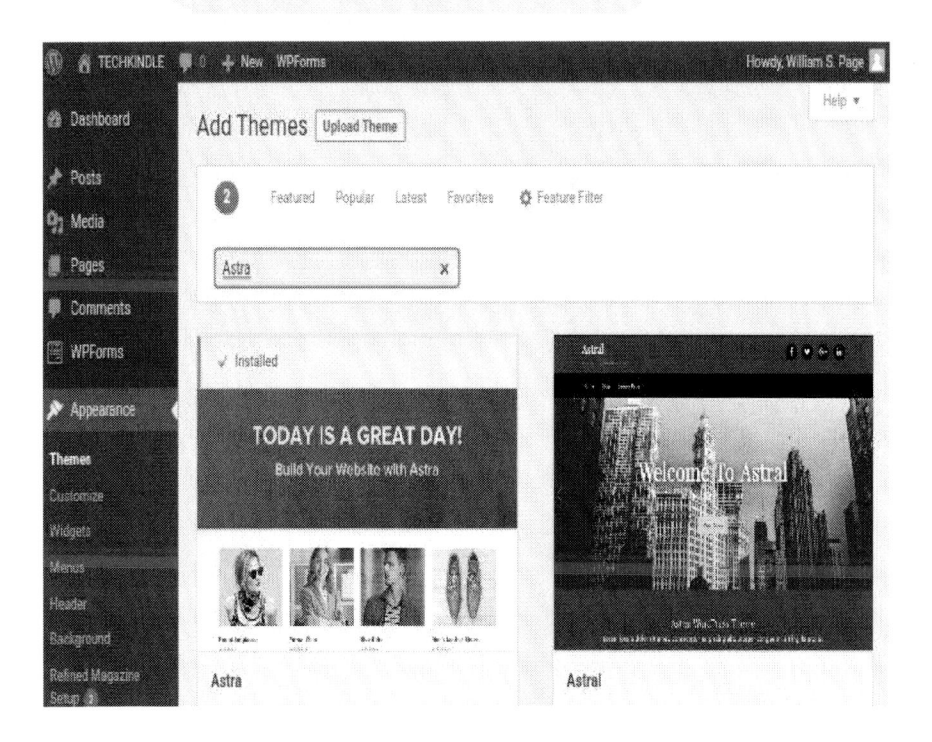

Fig 5.2: Searching for Theme Astra using theme search box

From the screenshot, you are to select the first theme. That is the one that has "TODAY IS A GREAT DAY!" written on its header. That is what we will be working with.

After you are done installing the theme known as Astra, the next thing is to activate it. If you do not activate the theme, it will not work on your website. So, take your mouse pointer/cursor up or your finger and hit activate depending on the kind of device you

92

are using.

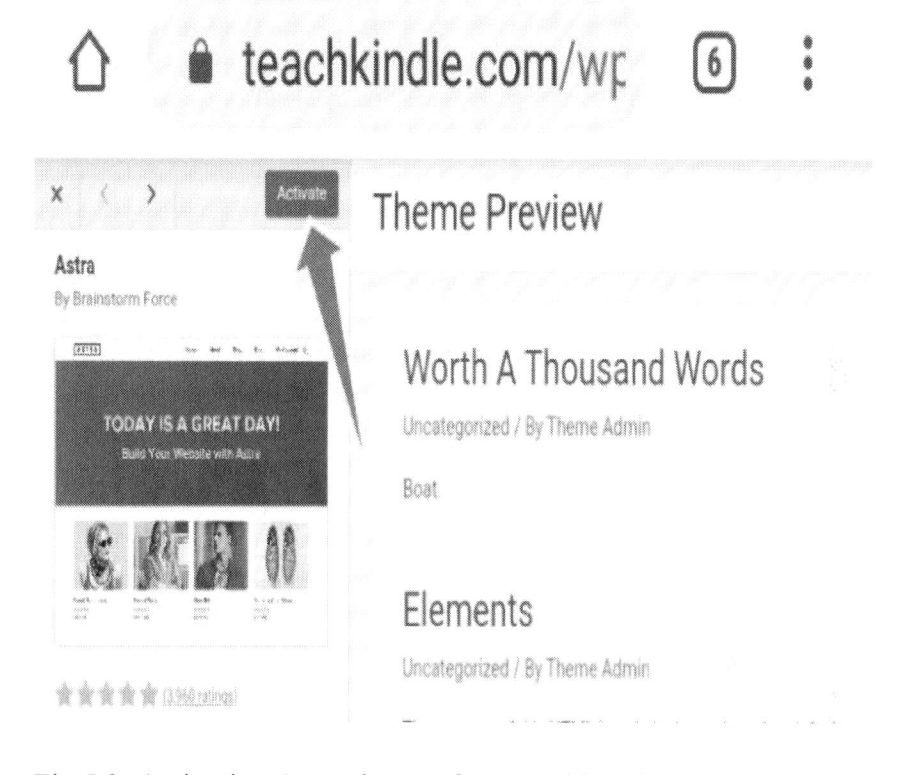

Fig 5.3: Activating Astra theme after searching through the box

Once the activation is done, then you are a little bit good to go. The system will instruct you in some cases to install some other software (plugins) to help the functionality of the theme. But if it does not, do not disturb yourself because I am here to help you.

Step 2: Installation of Plugin

As we have installed and activated the Astra theme, the next thing is to install the plugin that will help us work with the Astra theme. This gives us additional functionality to do what we want to do.

Go to the WordPress dashboard, then click on **plugins**. Among the sub options that shows when you clicked on the plugin in, select "**Add New**". A new page opens for you to search for the plugins you want to install.

In the Plugins search box, search for Astra. When it shows up, click on it, install and activate it. Astra plugin works with the theme.

Fig 5.4: Installation of Astra plugin

Also, I will like to inform you at this point that Astra Plugin has Elementor page builder integrated inside of it. That is why some website builders do not bother installing and activating Elementor plugin separately again once they have Astra Plugin already installed in their WordPress. But if you still install and activate elementor plugin separately irrespective of the fact that you already installed Astra plugin, it will not cause any conflict in WordPress system.

Note: Astra theme is different from Astra plugins, so follow my guide as I directed you.

Step 3: Choosing a Design

Astra plugin and elementor come with sets of designs. These designs are so many that you are left with a lot of choices on the one to use. Elementor is well built with stunning and stock designs. Some of the templates are free while some others are not.

To see and make your choice from these designs, from the dashboard screen options, select Plugins and then click on Installed Plugins. You will see the list of installed plugins in your dashboard. Scroll down, and you will see the one named "**Starter Templates**". Under the "**Starter Templates**" you will see "**See**

Library".

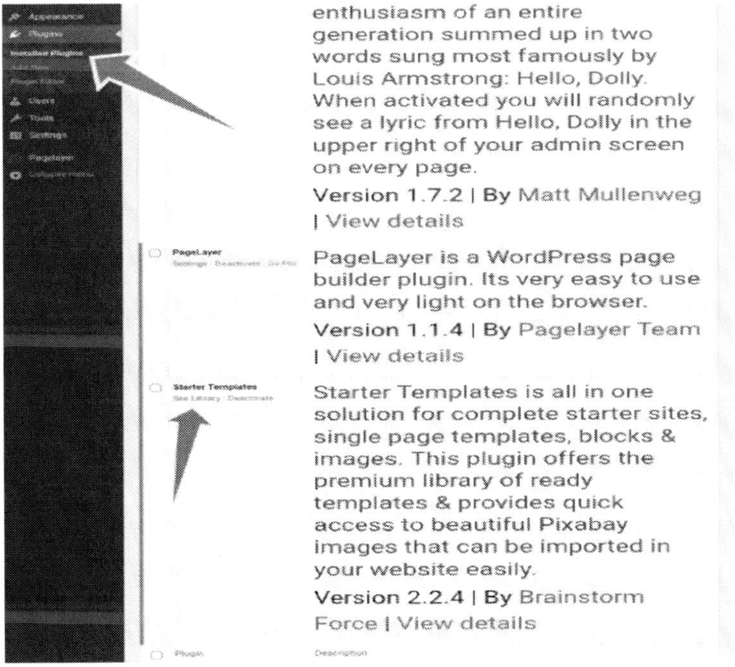
enthusiasm of an entire generation summed up in two words sung most famously by Louis Armstrong: Hello, Dolly. When activated you will randomly see a lyric from Hello, Dolly in the upper right of your admin screen on every page.
Version 1.7.2 | By Matt Mullenweg | View details
PageLayer is a WordPress page builder plugin. Its very easy to use and very light on the browser.
Version 1.1.4 | By Pagelayer Team | View details
Starter Templates is all in one solution for complete starter sites, single page templates, blocks & images. This plugin offers the premium library of ready templates & provides quick access to beautiful Pixabay images that can be imported in your website easily.
Version 2.2.4 | By Brainstorm Force | View details

Fig 5.5: Step to choose design from the installed Astra plugin

Click on the "**See Library**" and a new page will open showing different designs. At this point you are left with the option to choose any design.

Step 4: Selecting Page Builder

In step 3, we ended at clicking on "See Library" to select designs of your choice which can be achieved using any page builder software of Astra. As you click on the "See Library", you will be shown some page builders.

These page builders are Elementor, Breaver Builder, Gutenberg and Brizy. Without much stress, just select Elementor.

Fig 5.6: Selecting Elementor page builder after clicking on "See Library"

With the selection of this Elementor page builder, website building and design is made easy for us. It gives us flexibility to make edit of any text and images and we see how they change immediately at the landing page of our website. Not only landing page because you can select any page through menu and see how the changes occur as you edit.

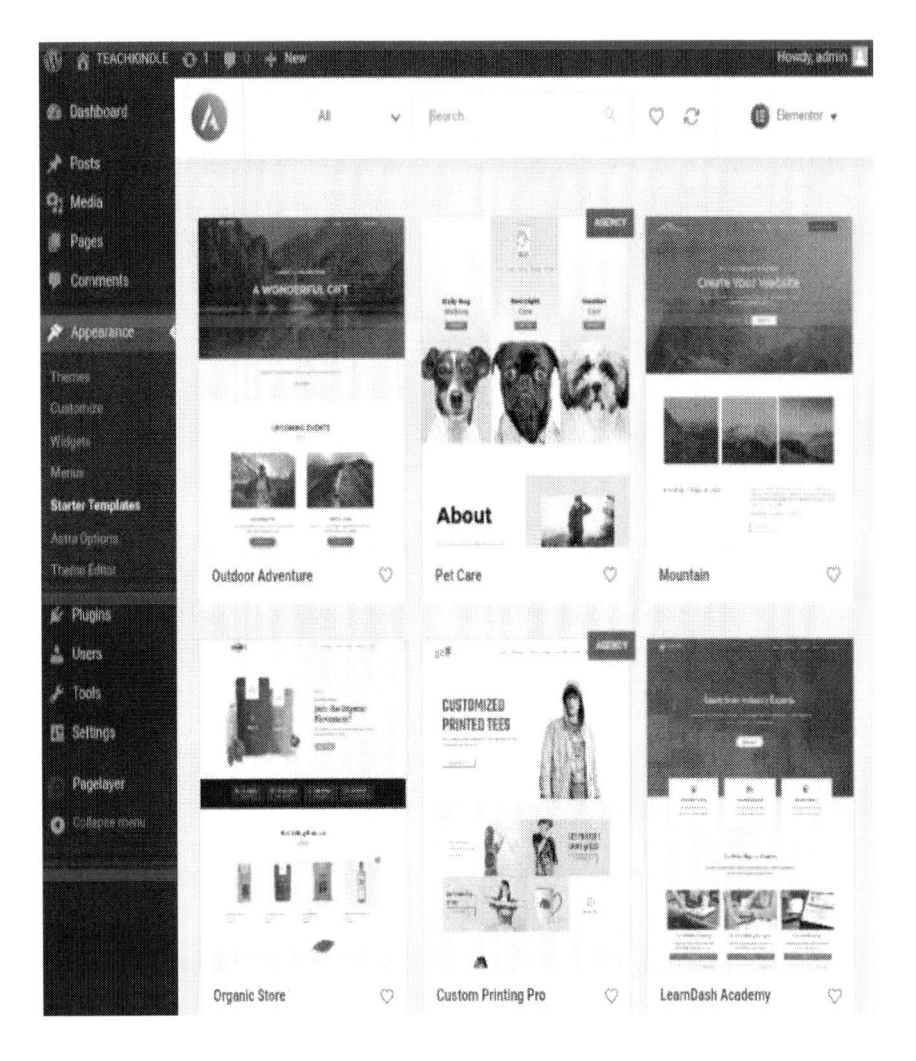

Fig 5.7: Next page showing different designs when Elementor is chosen

Out of those designs that will show up when you choose Elementor, you can choose any of them that you feel will be okay for your website. I want to bring to your notice that any of the designs tagged "Agency" are not free. So, choose any of the designs without that tag.

When you select any theme (a design) you will be shown how that design will look on your website. If you like the look, you can go on and install it. But if you do not like it, you can go back to the previous page and then choose another design. You can continue until you get your taste. But you change the template later.

Once you are okay with the one you found at last, you can use it to change the look of your website. This can apply to all your entire website or just the homepage of your website. It can even be applied only on a created page on your website. It is your choice to make. I will tell you how. The reason is because there are options for you on where you want the template to make remarkable change. There is "**Import Complete Site**" and "**Import "Home"** template options.

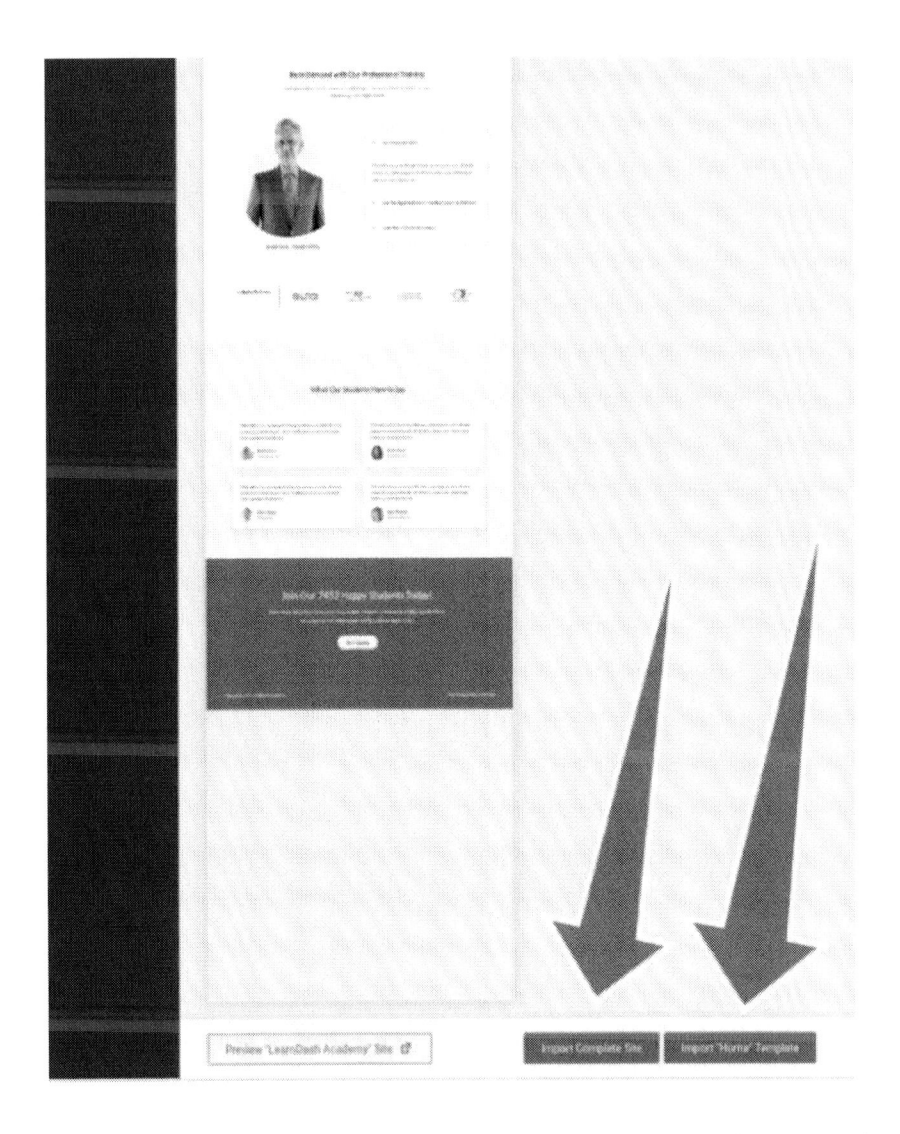

Fig 5.8: Choosing where you want your chosen template to make change

At this point let's work with making changes at the complete site entirely. So, select "Import Complete Site". This will help us to design our entire site including the homepage with the elementor template with changes applying to other pages of the website.

After selecting that option, there will be a pop up asking you to do the installation of the option you chose. Just go on with the installation. Once you complete the task, you will see a congratulatory message on your screen.

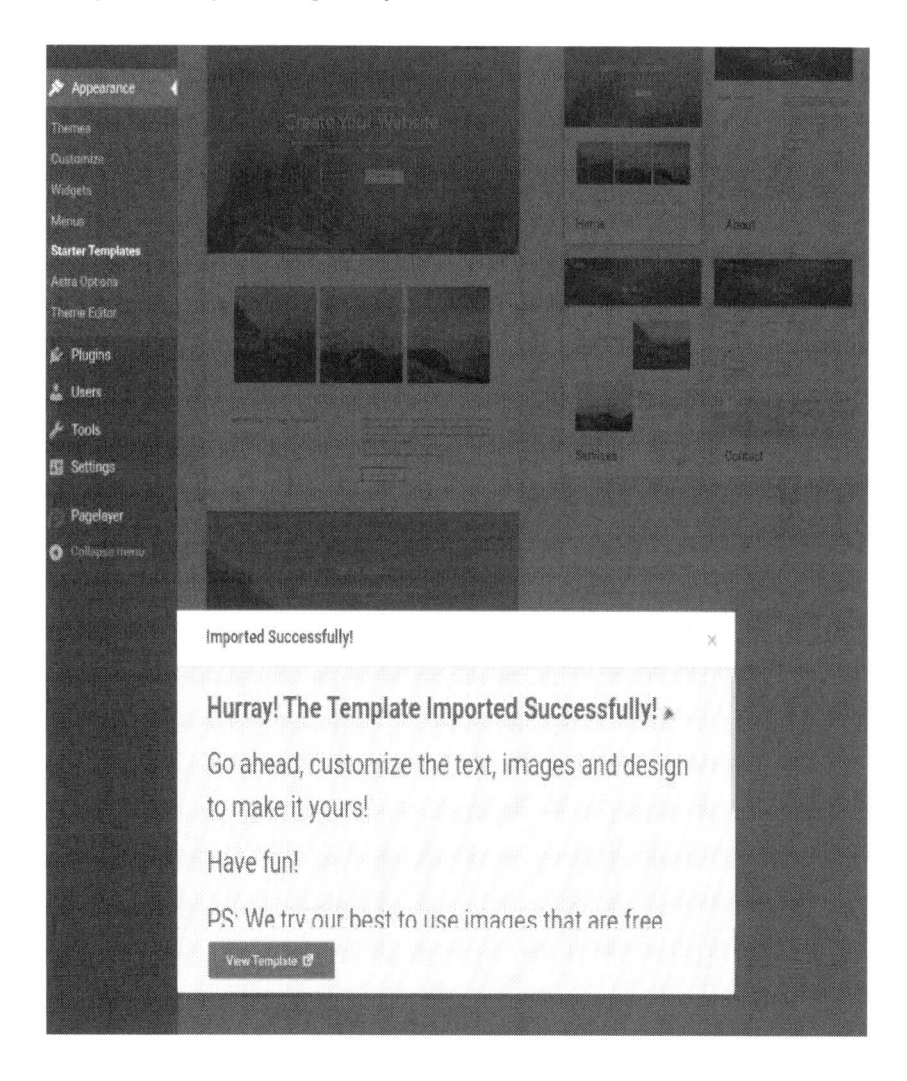

Fig 5.9: When you succeeded in importing the template from elementor

At this point, you can visit your website homepage and see the remarkable beautiful change on it. You will see nice background and other nice pictures. We will continue from next chapter.

Chapter 6

Building Website Pages

It is possible that after installing and activating any theme on your WordPress, you then find out that the theme does not show any pre-designed pages appearing as main menu items. That is to say that the website will not show menu items like "Home", "About", "Contact", "Services" and "Blog" on it.

Fig 6: A website without menu items formed from pages

From the image of Fig 6, there is no menu items or navigation menu bars at the header section of the website. It is so because it has not been added on the website. I will teach you how you can add it to give visitors to your website opportunity to check through many places on your website and keep them engaged.

In blog sites, adding pages that will display as navigation menu items as possible is avenue to get more people to read more of your published contents. Maybe you have menu items like Sports and another as entertainment, someone may finish reading something new on Sports and decide to go for Entertainment menu bar. As he does this, you are getting more views on your website and creating more chances for visitors to click on ads placed on your website and you make money when that happens.

What are the Pages we will be Creating?

In this teaching, I will be teaching you how to create the following pages:

- Home

- Contact

- About

- Services and

- Blog

Step by Step Guide in Creation Home Page with Elementor and Adding it to Main Menu

To complete this task, take the following steps:

- Login to your WordPress admin dashboard

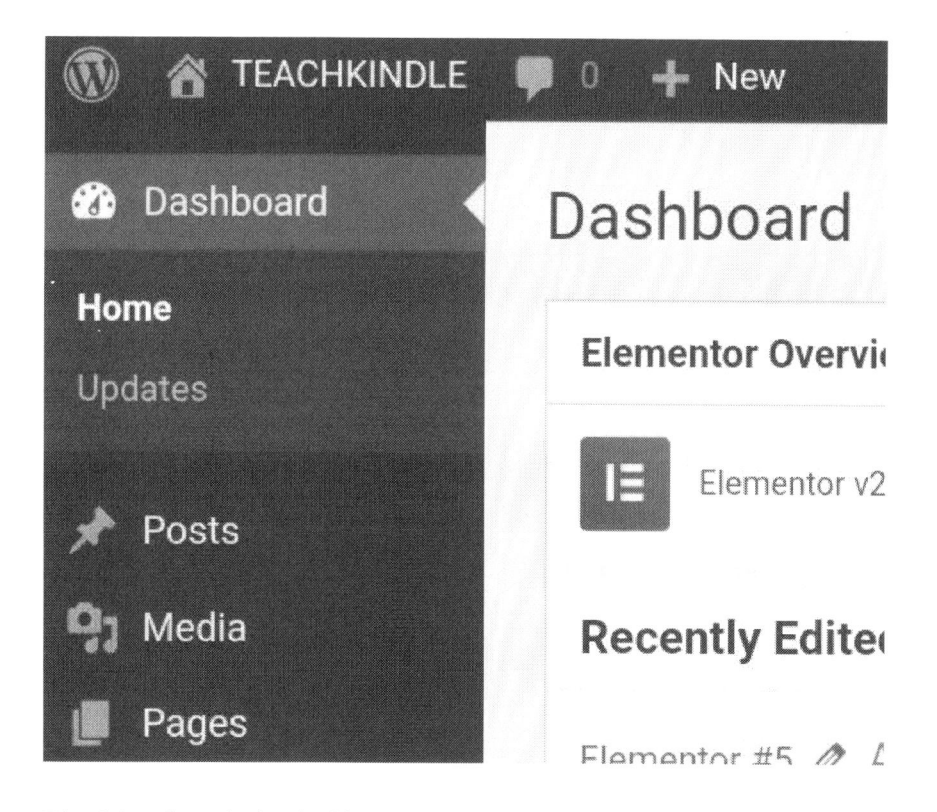

Fig 6.1: The admin dashboard of my WordPress account

- Open a new tab in that same browser you used to login to your

WordPress admin dashboard

- Type the URL of your website and search.

Example I am to visit my website www.teachkindle.com if that is the site am building

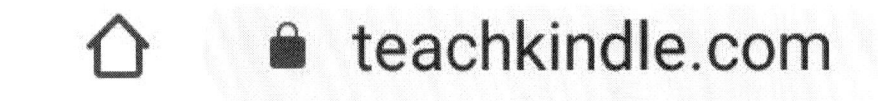

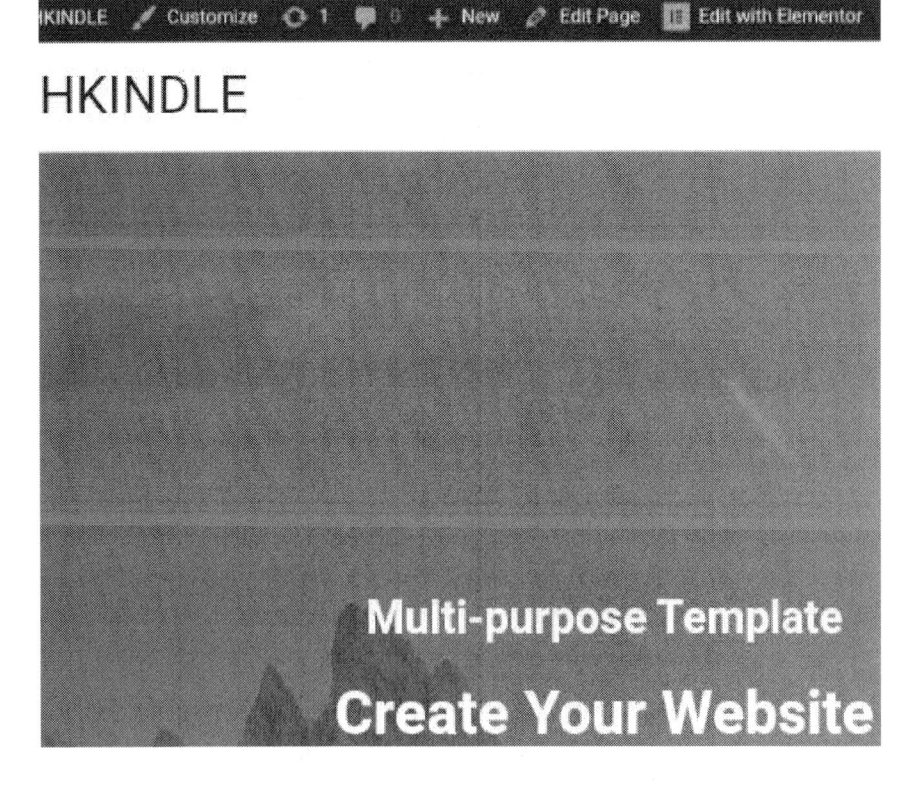

Fig 6.2: The landing page of my teaching site www.teachkindle.com

- Click on the "+ New" tab by the top left corner of your site and select "Page" as some options display

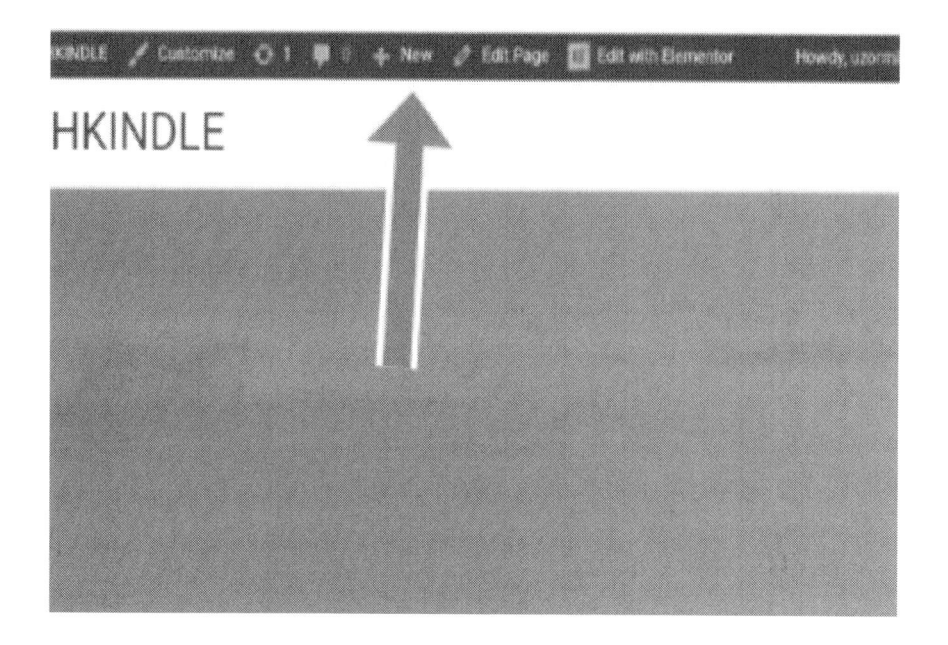

Fig 6.3: Select the "+ New" tab as shown

- Select Edit with Elementor

As the Page which you selected opens, look at the top and you will see "Edit with Elementor", just click on it and give your page title, which is "Home"

Fig 6.4: Edit with Elementor shown

- Name that page title as Home

- Click on Publish to Save your website Home

Fig 6.5: The position of Publish button

As you click on Publish, you have saved your created page

Step by Step Guide in Adding the Home Page as a Main Menu Item

To add the already created page as a menu item so that it displays on top of your website, do the following:

- Login to your WordPress admin dashboard

- Click on Appearance

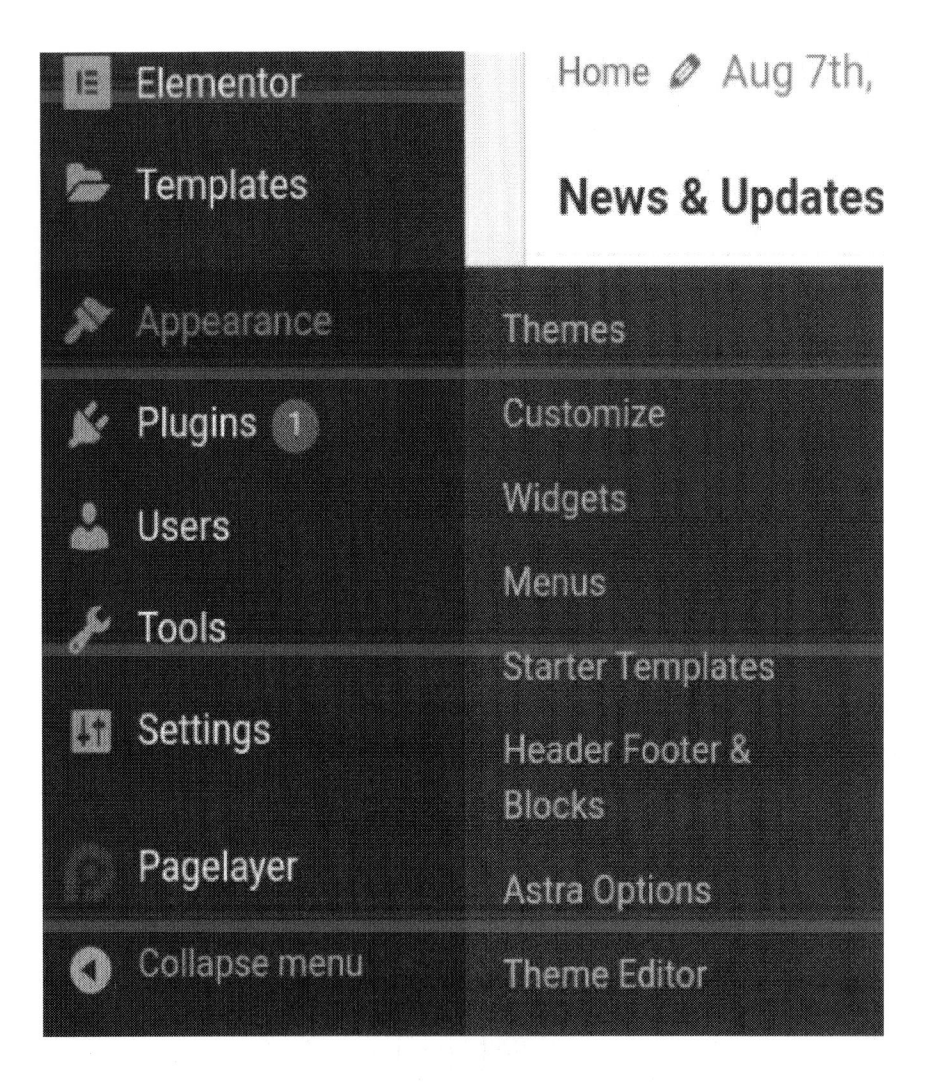

Fig 6.6: When Appearance is clicked on

-Select Customize

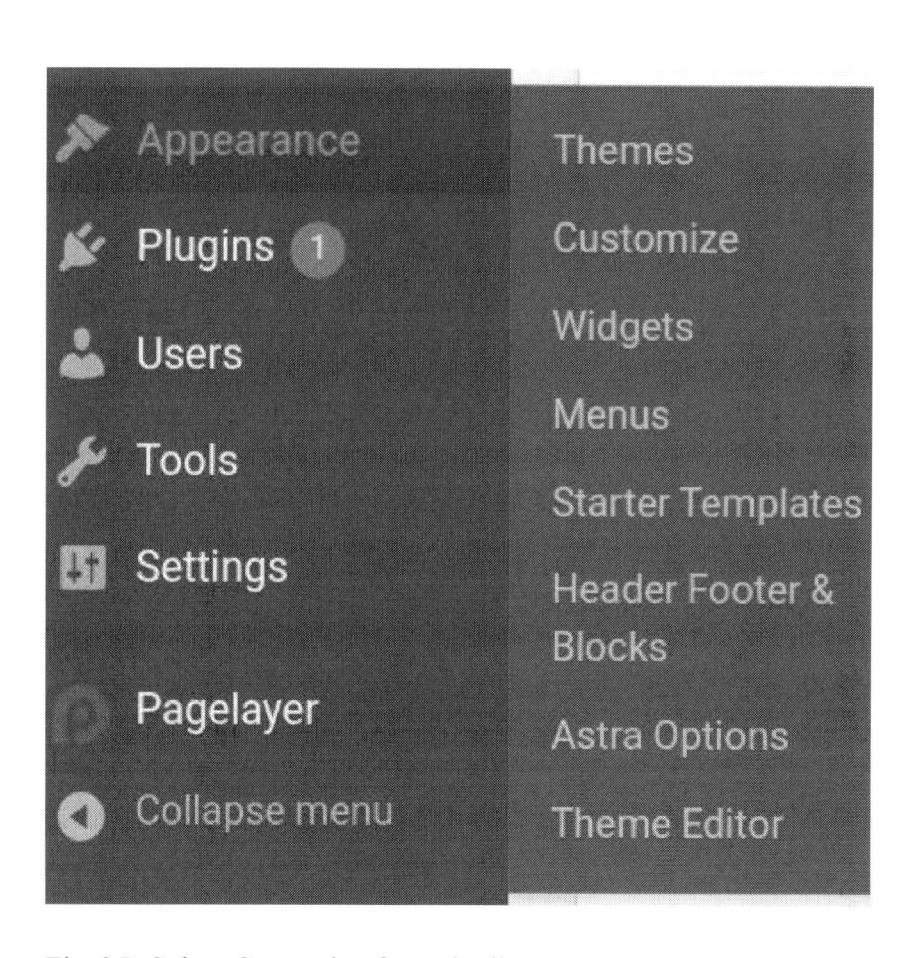

Fig 6.7: Select Customize from the list

- Select Menus

You are customizing

TEACHKINDLE

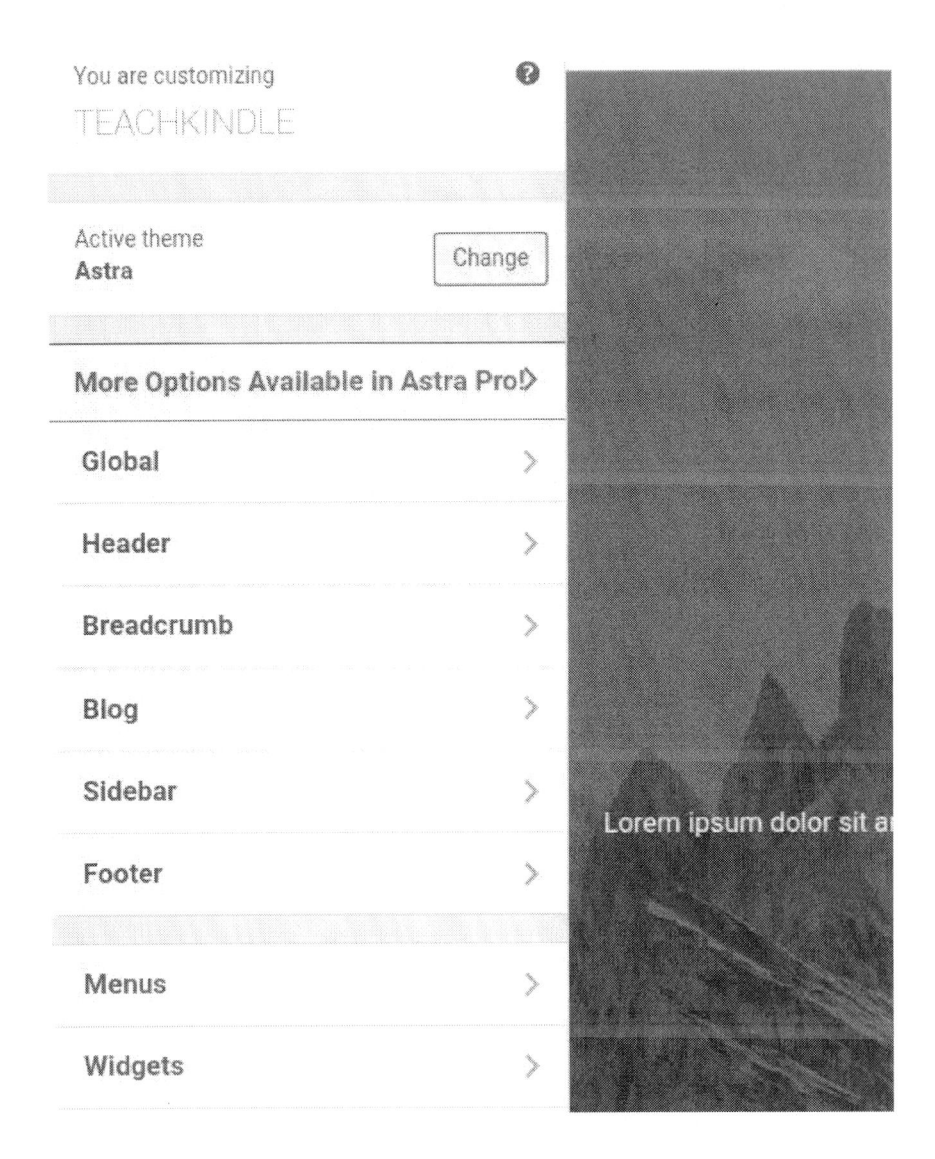

Active theme
Astra   [Change]

More Options Available in Astra Pro

Global >

Header >

Breadcrumb >

Blog >

Sidebar >

Footer >

Menus >

Widgets >

Fig 6.8: Select Menus from the list

-Click on Main menu or Navigation menu depending on the term in use by your system

When the page opens after you selected Menus, click on the main

menu

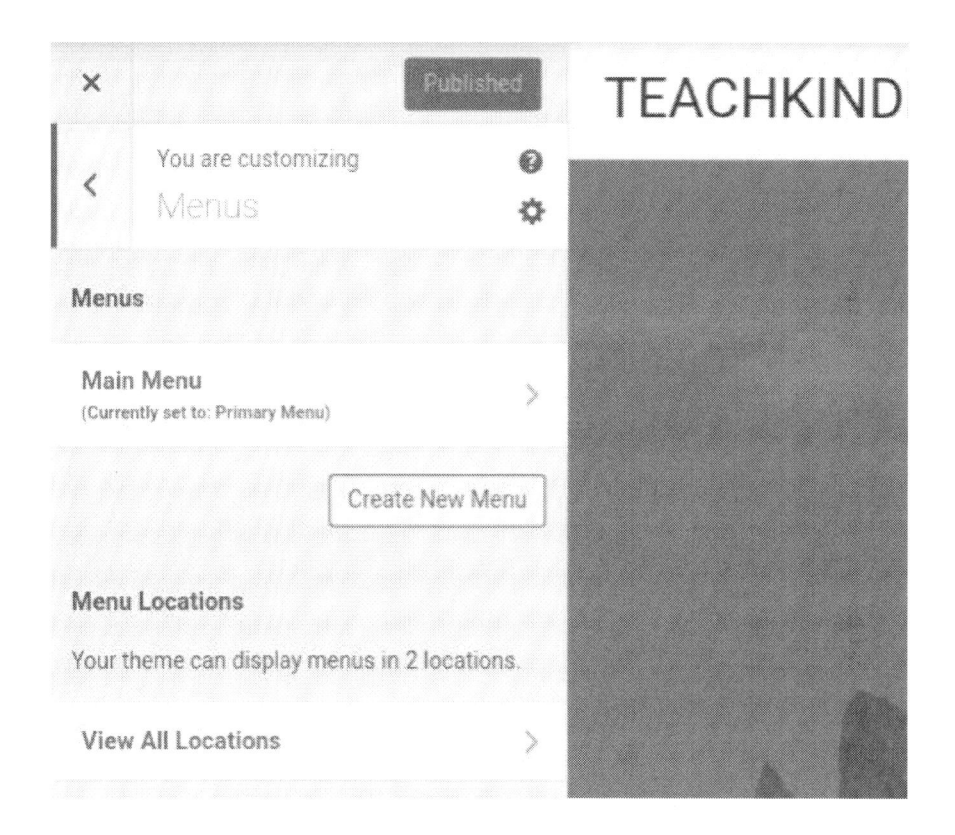

Fig 6.9: I will click on main menu if am designing with this term

As you clicked on the Main Menu, a new page opens. This page allows you to add that page you have created before which is "Home" page

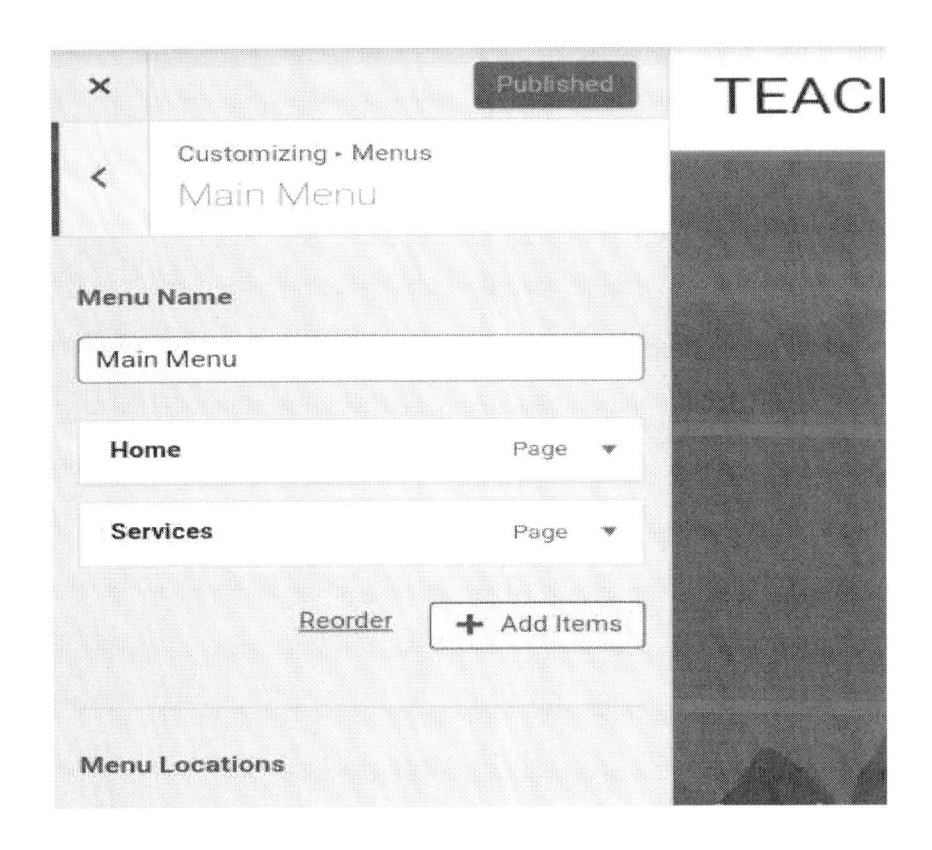

Fig 6.1.1: The new page that opened

-Click on the +Add items, search for the home menu which will appear by the right, select it to be added among the main menu items

-Click on the Publish button after the page is added to save the added items.

Save it by hitting publish button.

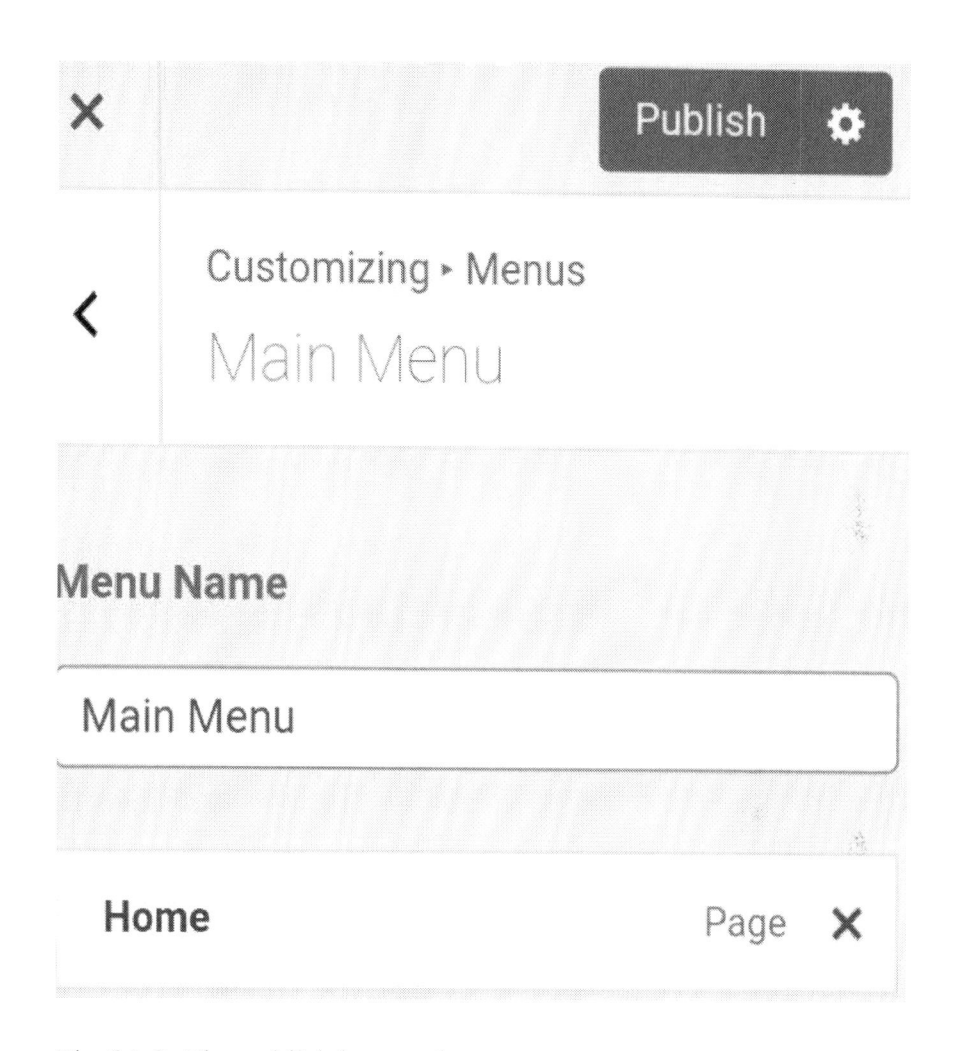

Fig 6.1.2: The publish button shown

The Publish button is at the top. So, click on it to save the changes.

Step by Step Guide in Creating "Contact" Page

Contact page is a page on any website that gives visitors

information on how to contact a person that owns the website or the company. It can include contact form, the address of the company, the social media links of the company or the owner, phone number and the email Address.

Creating Contact page is the same step to the way I taught you in creating a website Home page using elementor. Also, to add it as a menu item so it appears in main menu, it is the same steps

To create the "Contact" page using elementor, take the following steps:

- Login to your WordPress admin dashboard

- Open a new tab in that same browser you used to login to your WordPress admin dashboard

- Type the URL of your website and search

- Click on the "+ New" tab by the top left corner of your site and select "Page" as some options display

- Add your title as Contact

- Select Edit with Elementor

You will see this Edit with Elementor when the page opened after selecting "Page" in the previous step

Fig 6.1.3: Edit with Elementor shown

- Click on Publish to Save your website "Contact" page

Step by Step Guide in Adding the Contact Page as a Main Menu Item

To add the already created page as a menu item so that it displays on top of your website, do the following:

- Login to your WordPress admin dashboard

- Click on Appearance

- Select Customize

- Select Menus

-Click on Main menu or Navigation menu depending on the term in use by your system

- Select "+Add Items" tab.

This will open some pages already created by you or the system.

Fig 6.1.4: Click on the tab to be allowed to add Contact page

- Select the "Contact" page from the list of Already created Pages that may appear

119

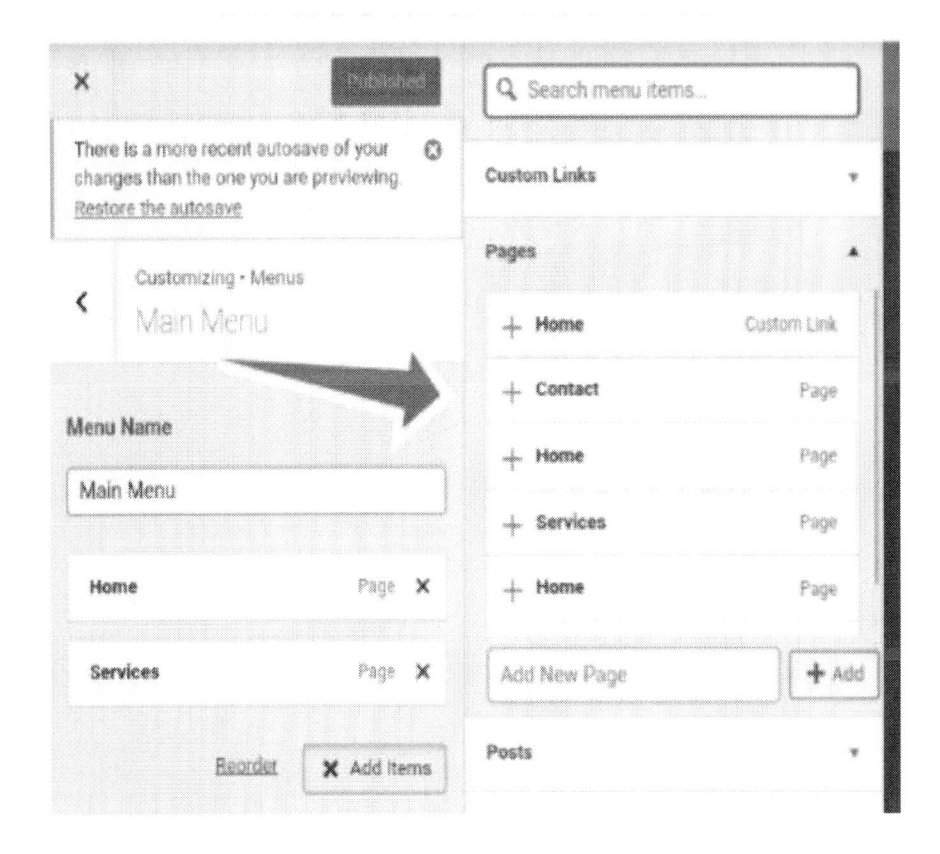

Fig 6.1.5: Selecting the "Contact" Page from the list

Once you select the Contact, it will be moved to the Main Menu or Navigation menu section. At this point, the "Publish" button shows brighter blue color

- Click on the "Publish"

This will publish the new page you just added

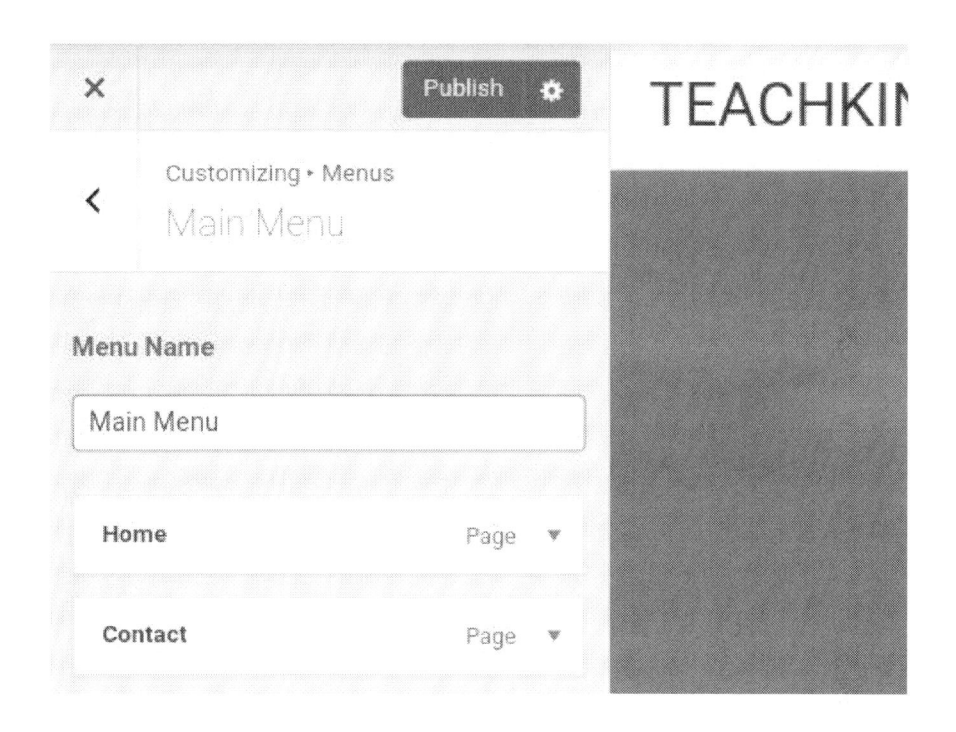

Fig 6.1.6: The Publish button shows brighter blue color located on top

You can visit your website and see how the added page item appears with others.

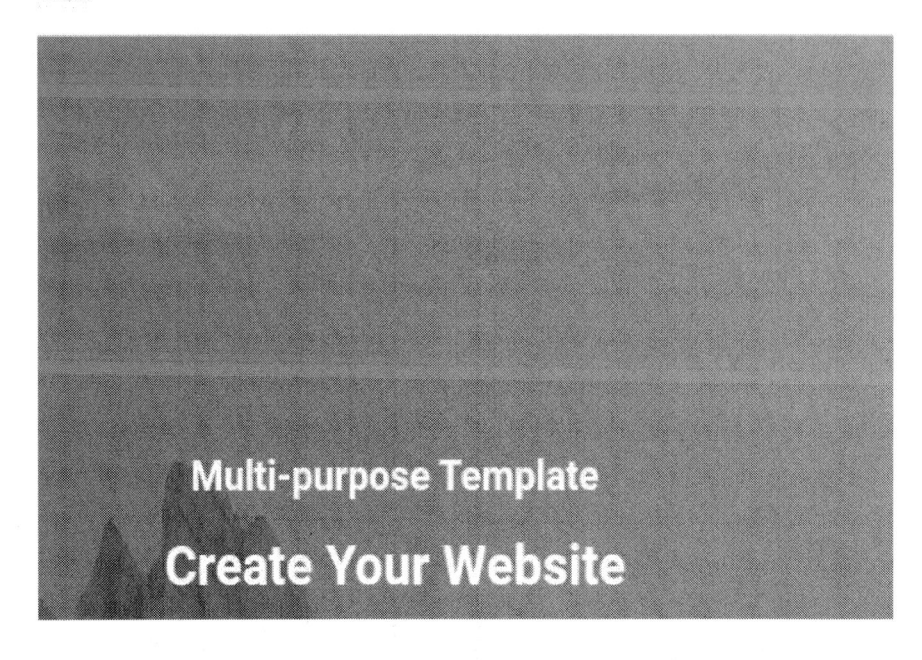

Fig 6.1.7: My website landing page showing the just created and added "Contact" page along with the first created "Home" page

Step by Step Guide in Creating "About" Page

The same steps I taught you to use to create Home and Contact pages is the same steps you need to create "About" Page for your website. About page tells visitors basics about your website. It can tell people history of your company that the website is created for and the accolades the company has earned over the years.

I am stopping my teaching on creating webpages in "About" page and from here you can add as many pages as possible to your website and from there design beautiful pages with elementor when the time comes.

To create About page on your website, take the following steps:

- Login to your WordPress admin dashboard

- Open a new tab in that same browser you used to login to your WordPress admin dashboard

- Type the URL of your website and search

- Click on the "+ New" tab by the top left corner of your site and select "Page" as some options will display

- Add your title as "About"

- Select Edit with Elementor

As the page loads and opens showing elementor building tools, just go back to the page you were before by punching the back button on your computer or using your computer mouse and you will be taken back to this page below:

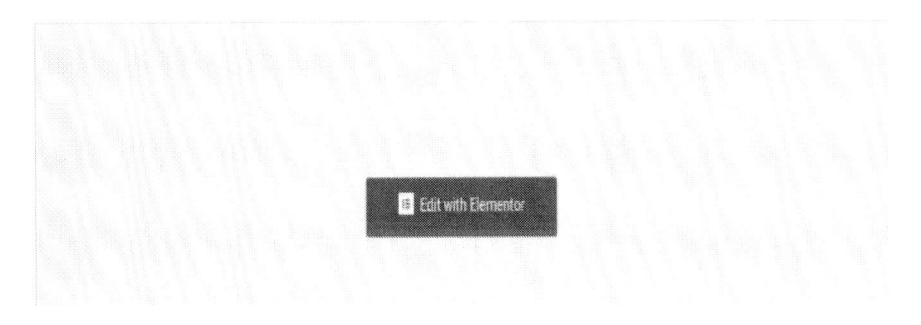

Fig 618: The creating of About Page

- Click on Publish to publish your website "About" page

Step by Step Guide in Adding the Created "About" Page to Navigation Menu as Menu Item

- Login to your WordPress admin dashboard

- Click on Appearance

- Select Customize

- Select Menus

-Click on Main menu or Navigation menu depending on the term in use by your system

- Select "+Add Items" tab.

This will open some pages already created by you or the system.

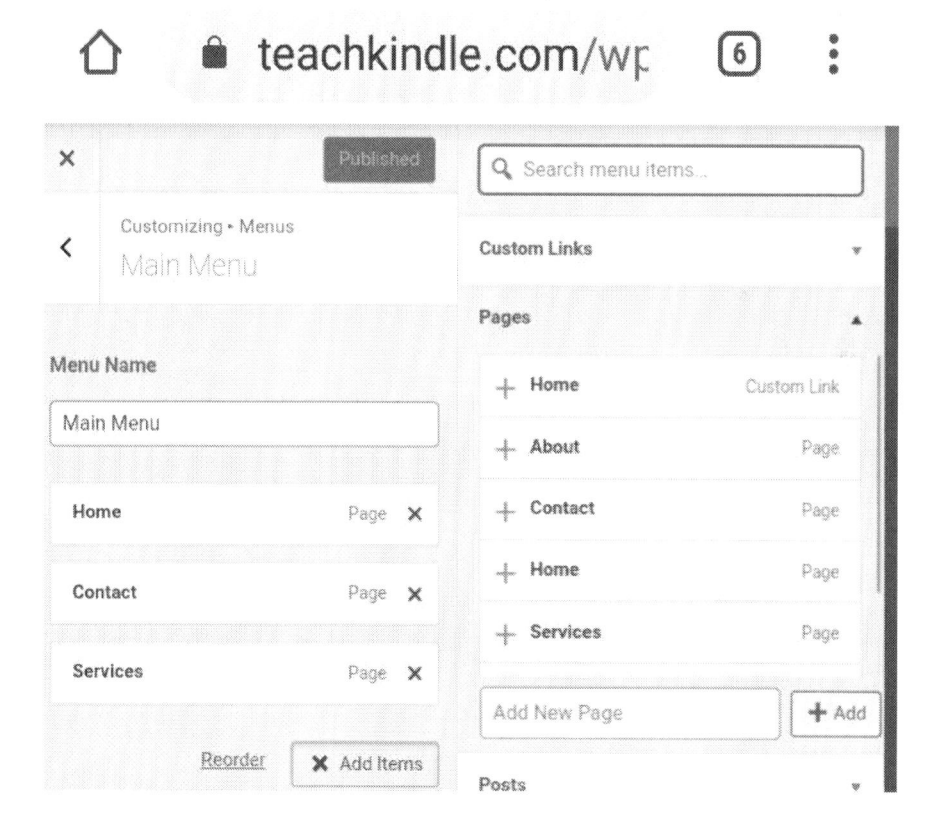

Fig 6.1.9: Page that opened when I selected "+Add Items" tab.

- Select the "About" page from the list of already created pages that will appear

- Click on the "Publish"

When you click on "Publish" the About is published on your website.

With this teaching, I have taught you how you can create pages on your website. You can create the two remaining pages "Blog" and "Services" with this my teaching. We will get to the section where I will teach you have to design these pages using elementor page builder.

Note: There are still other methods you can use to create pages. So, if you have a book that taught you another way to complete the same task, that is carried also.

More Importantly: If you run into any issue, do well to write to me.

Chapter 7

Footer Design with Elementor

Elementor makes it possible for us to be able to design the footer areas of our websites. In this chapter, I will be teaching you how to design your website footer section. It is a step by step guide that will help you create stunning website footer section. So, without taking much time, let us begin.

How to build the Footer Contents with Elementor

To build the footer content of a website, take the following steps:

- Login to your WordPress admin area or visit your WordPress homepage

You must first sign into your WordPress admin area first. That is the first step you must take before going into other steps.

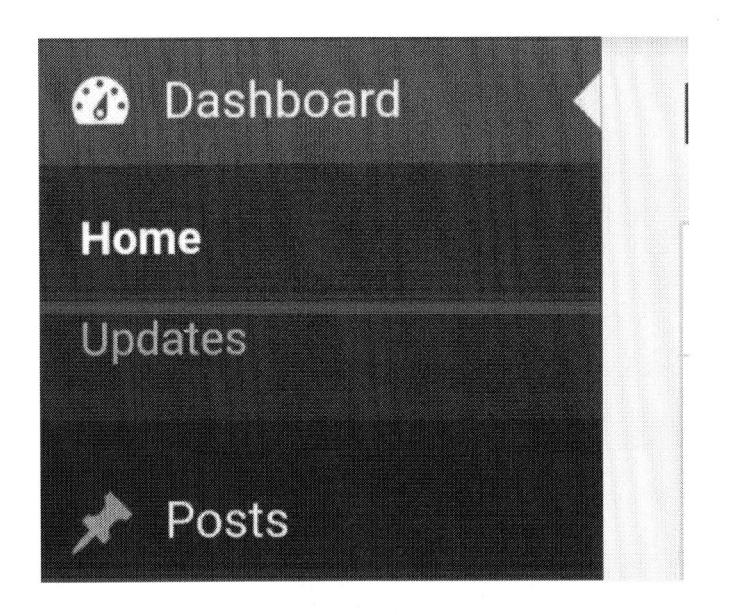

Fig 7: The homepage of my WordPress admin area

- Open a new tab in your browser and then visit your website homepage or the menu item page you want to design

Do not forget you must first sign into your WordPress admin area before you open a new tab in the same browser and then visit your website. If I am to design the website I am using for this teaching, I will visit www.teachkindle.com in this stage in a new tab in the same browser

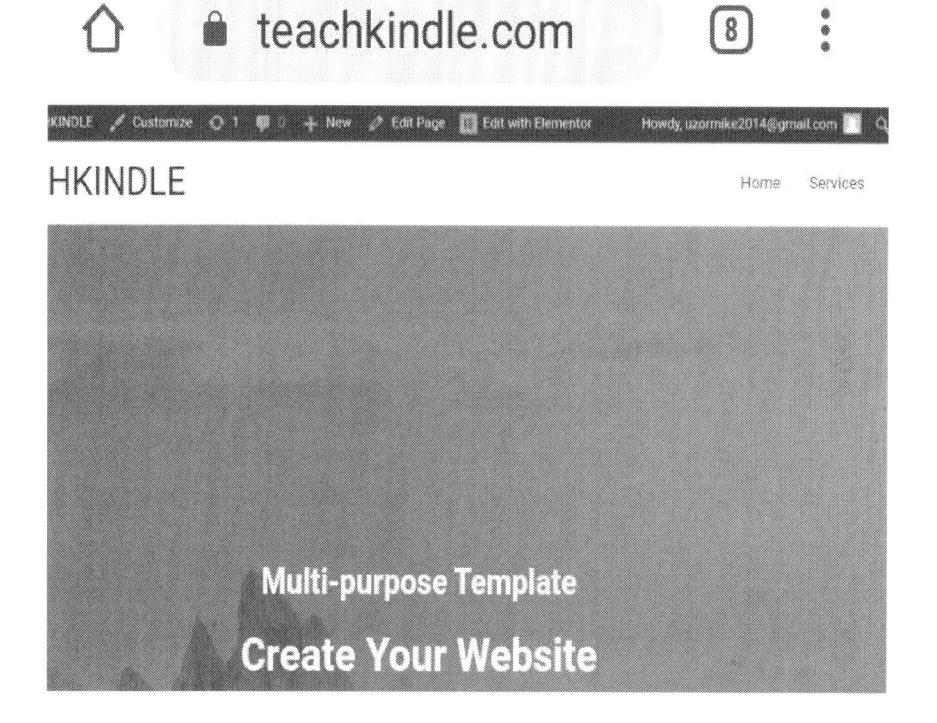

Fig 7.1: Picture shows my website homepage when I visited in new tab

From the picture above, the Home, which I want to design its footer area is designed in blue color.

- Click on Edit with Elementor

Edit with Elementor tab is at the top part of your website homepage or page menu item you want to build its footer section

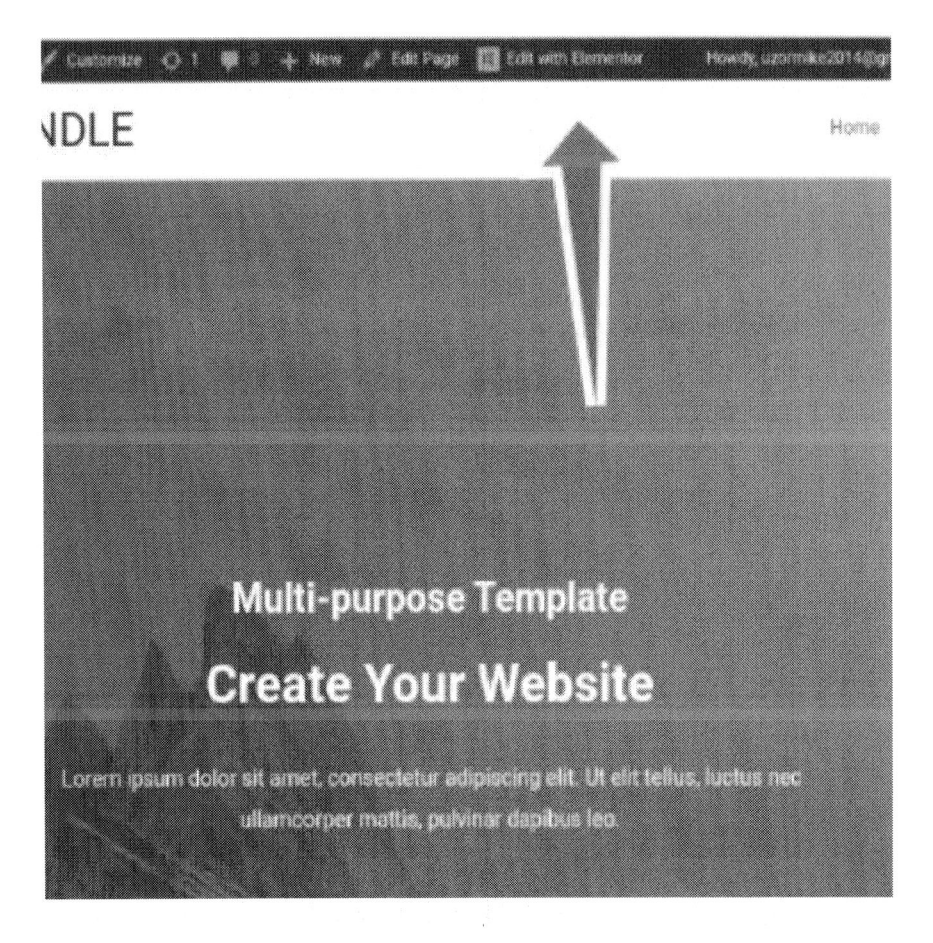

Fig 7.2: Edit with Elementor at the top part of your website

- Select the Astra symbol as the new page opens

When you click on Edit with Elementor, a new page opens. From that page that opens, select either the elementor (+) or Astra symbol. Do not forget we are building this page with Astra theme and Elementor. So, you must have installed and activated the Astra theme and plugin.

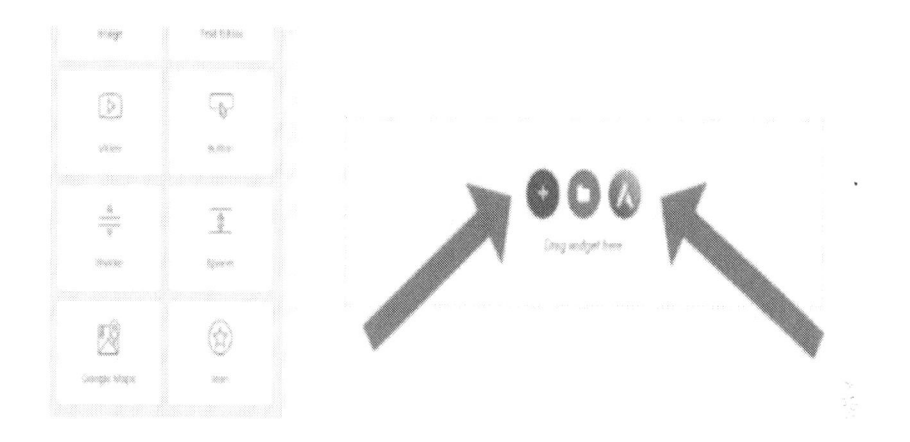

Fig 7.3: Select either the elementor (+) or Astra Symbol to choose any template from elementor

This will give you room to choose from the series of elementor footer templates. You can also decide to just click on the plus symbol (+) in read instead of the Astra Symbol.

-As you select any of the options, a new window opens which allows you to choose any footer predesigned template

As for me I will choose and import any block or page footer design that I know will match my footer template section. Please do not just import the whole template. You will see sections like "About" and "Contact". If you know any of them that you believe will be fine on your site, just choose it.

131

Fig 7.4: Choosing predesignated template that will likely fit your site footer

If after seeing the footer template when you visit your website and it does not suit the design, just go back and change it.

Note: You must have created Pages on your website through the WordPress Page screen option before you can then start the design of the footer area of your website.

Next: Designing the Footer Template After Import

This is the last stage of my website footer section design in this teaching using elementor page builder. As you have imported and saved the template, the next is the concluding part of the stage. So, to conclude the design with elementor, do the following?

-Login to your WordPress dashboard if you have not done so or if you logged out

-Open a new tab in that your same browser and visit the webpage you want to build with elementor

- Select "Edith with Elementor" from the top part of your website

- Then as the window loads and opens, scroll down to the footer section of your website where you want to change the default words that came with the template, change images if available and then add the possible links you want to add.

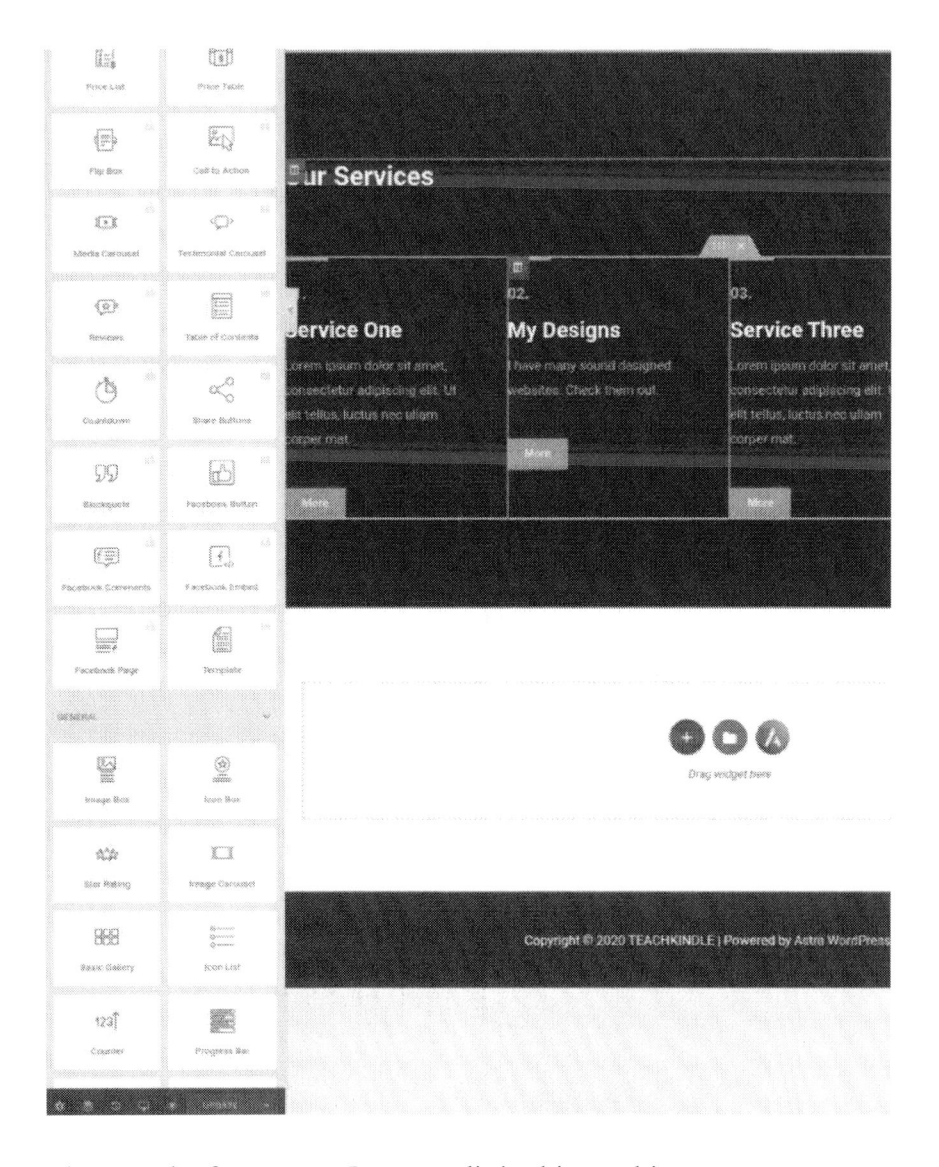

Fig 7.5: The footer area I am to edit in this teaching

As you click on any part of that footer area, you can make some possible changes. After making the changes to your taste, just click on the "Update" left-hand corner of the site, and the changes you made will be saved. As you make your typing in the provided space at the footer section, what you type are shown up inside the box at the top left-hand corner. If you make any mistake at the end of the design, you can edit that part again following my previous guide.

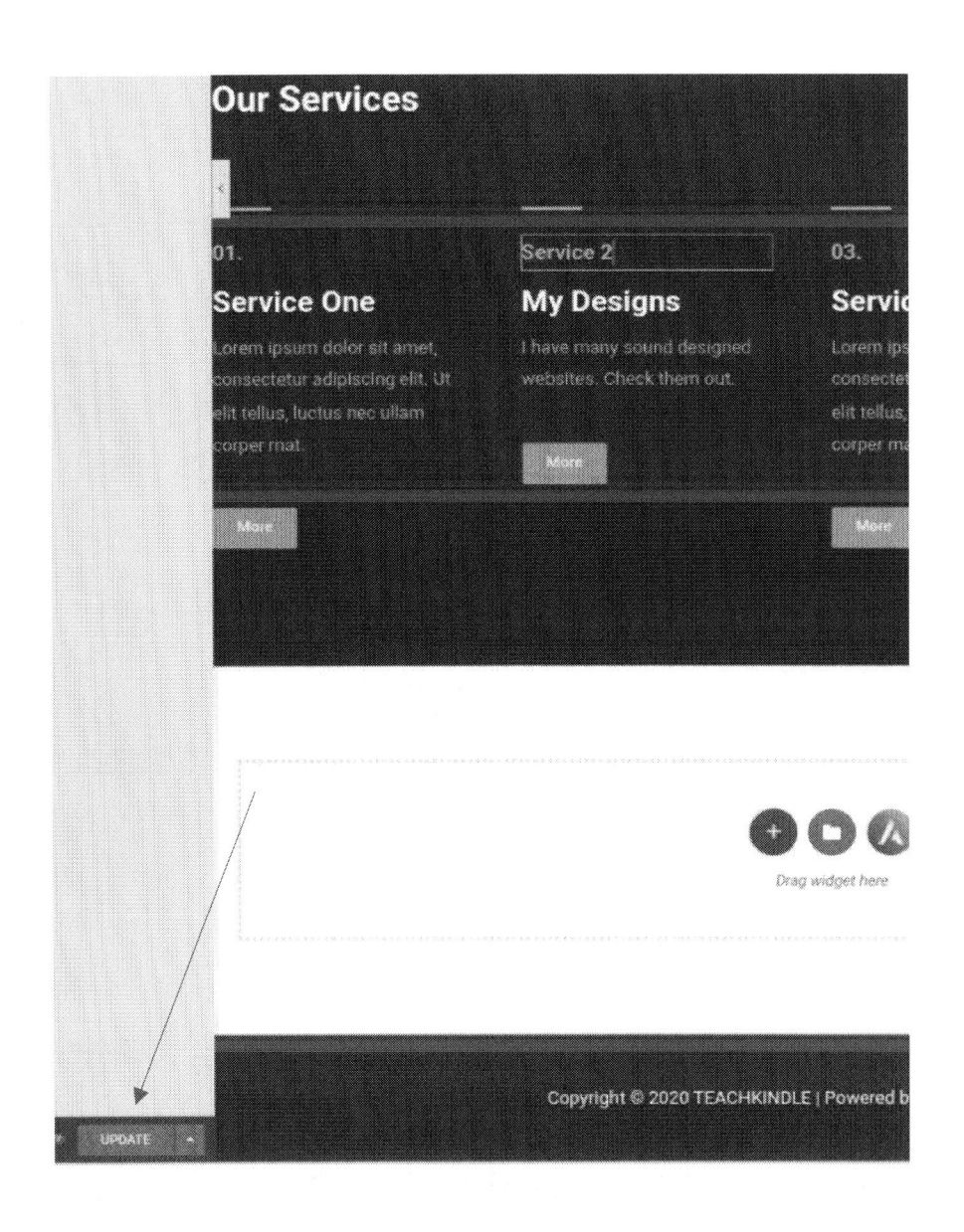

Fig 7.6: Click on the "Update" to save changes made

Building Social Media Links at Footer with Elementor

You may ask how possible it is for you to build social media links at the footer section of your website using elementor. But it is possible and there are ways it can be done. You can decide to build with the already pre-designed social media links on the footer area of your website or you can important footer template only with the help of your elementor and then edit Added the links that will take the visitors to your social media pages.

The truth is that I am here to make you happy by giving you first class teaching on how to insert social media links to the footer area of your website. There are many ways you can do this with elementor but am teaching you with one of them which seems to be the easiest among all. Do not hesitate to write to me if any challenge comes up. I am here to teach you. My email is on one of the last pages of this book.

Step by Step Guide in Adding Social Media Links to the Footer Area of your Website using Elementor

The steps are like the one we used in Editing the footer area of a website which I discussed in the previous subheading. The only remarkable change is when I will add the social media links and logos. When you become an expert, you will bypass some of all these steps.

To add the links, take these steps:

- Login to your WordPress dashboard if you have not done so or if you logged out

- Open a new tab in that your same browser and visit the webpage you want to integrate its footer part with social media links using elementor

- Click on Edit with Elementor

- Scroll down to the bottom part where you want to integrate the links

- Click on any part of the footer where you want to edit and add the links

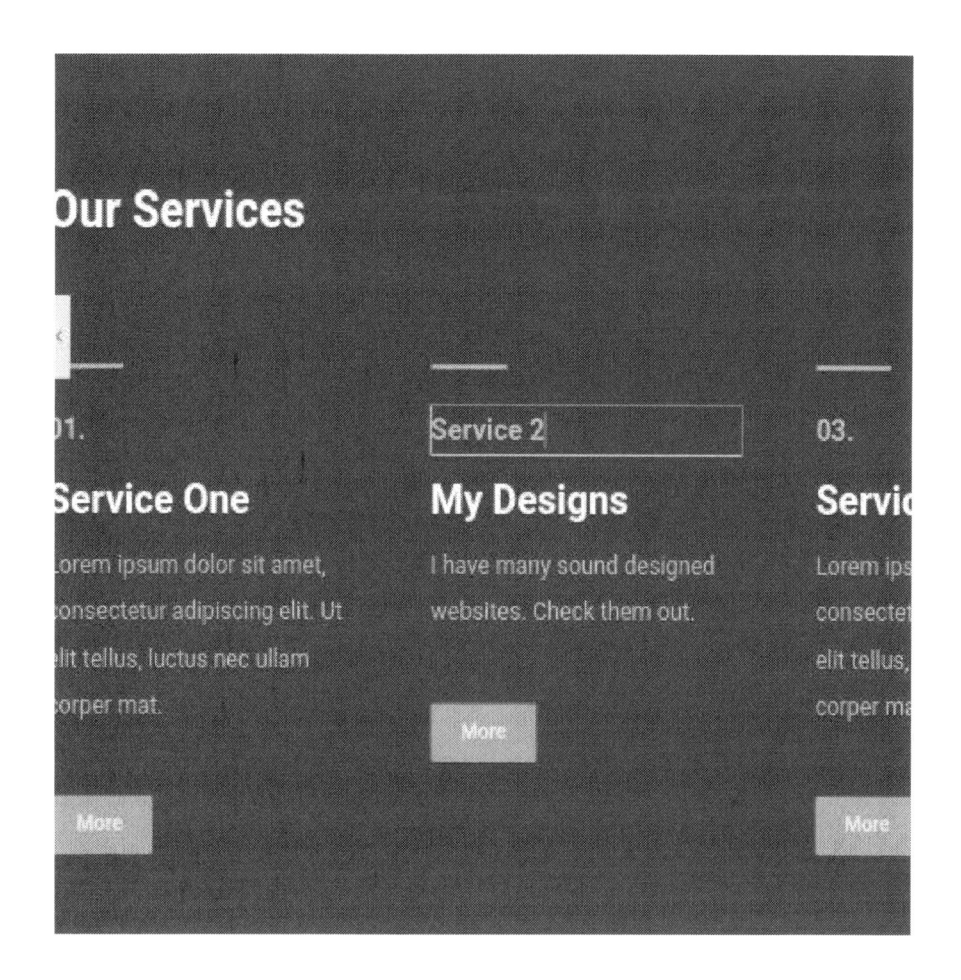

Fig 7.7: The footer area to add the social media link

Note: This entire footer area can be duplicated from that which we used to design in the previous subheading I titled "Next: Designing the Footer Template After Import". That is one of the beauties of building with elementor. You can also take the step of importing that same footer template and them make your changes to use the last one for footer social media links.

- Start making your change

As you click on the area you want to make you change, erase the unnecessary word on it and add your own words. That will match that area.

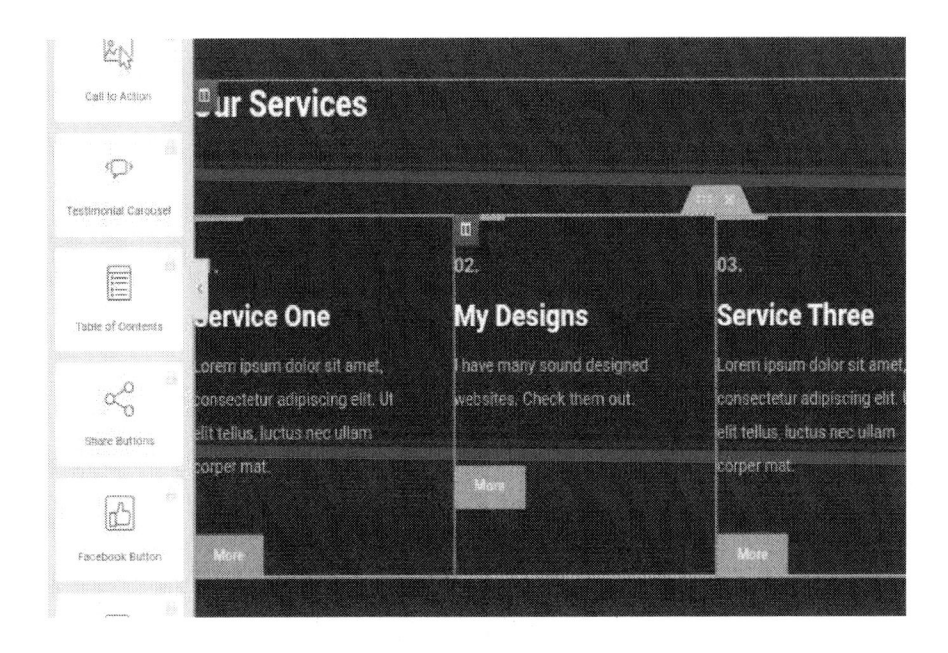

Fig 7.8: Possible areas to make your change

Example you can use "Our Facebook Link" as a title of the Facebook link. Then add few words like "Connect with us on Facebook" as few statements to let the people know what the link is all about.

- Under Content in the Icon part, type "Facebook" and then select the Facebook Icon you want to use

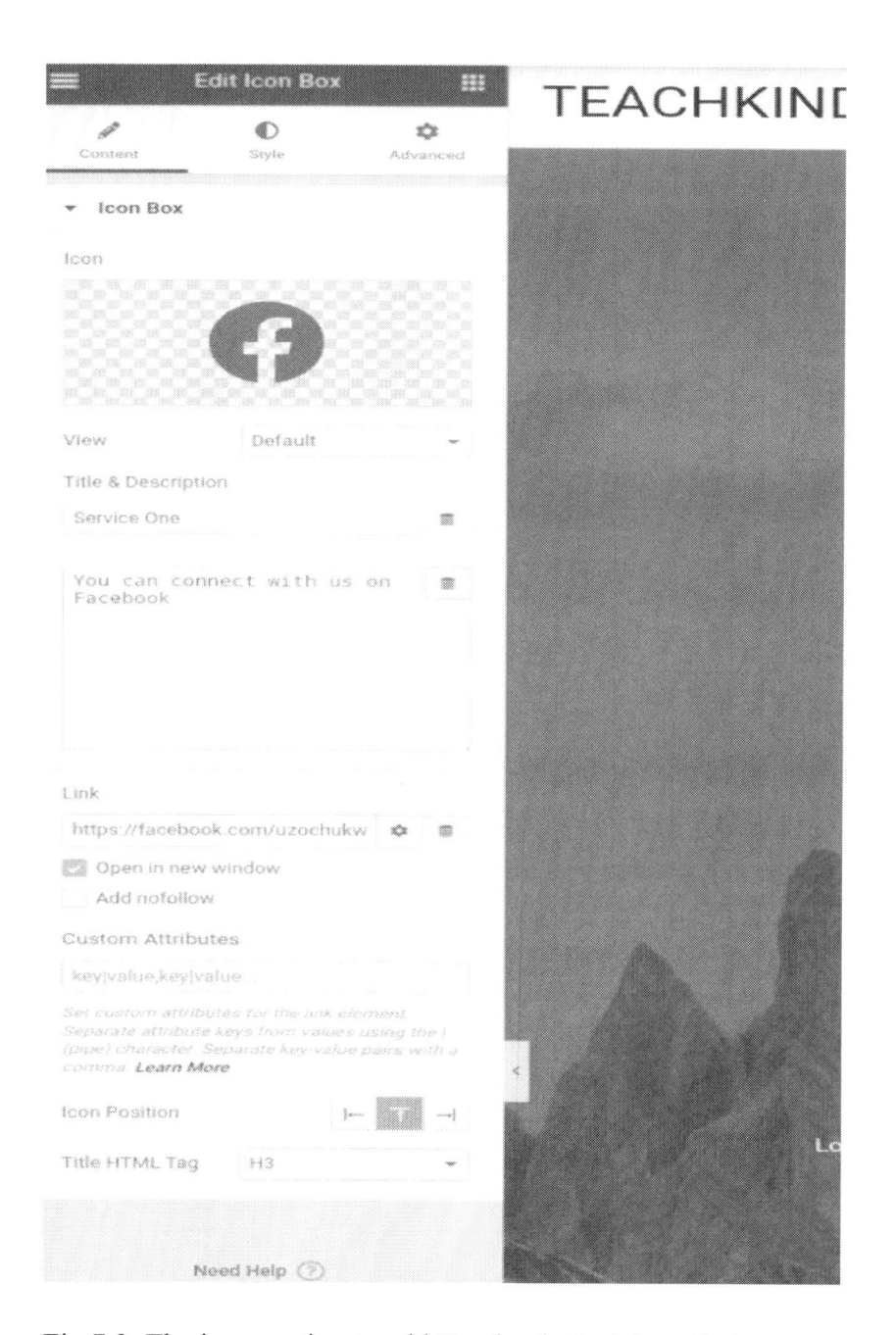

Fig 7.9: The icon section to add Facebook Social media icon

141

- Add the link to the Facebook page. This is the link you want visitors to your website to visit when they click on it so they can follow your social media page.

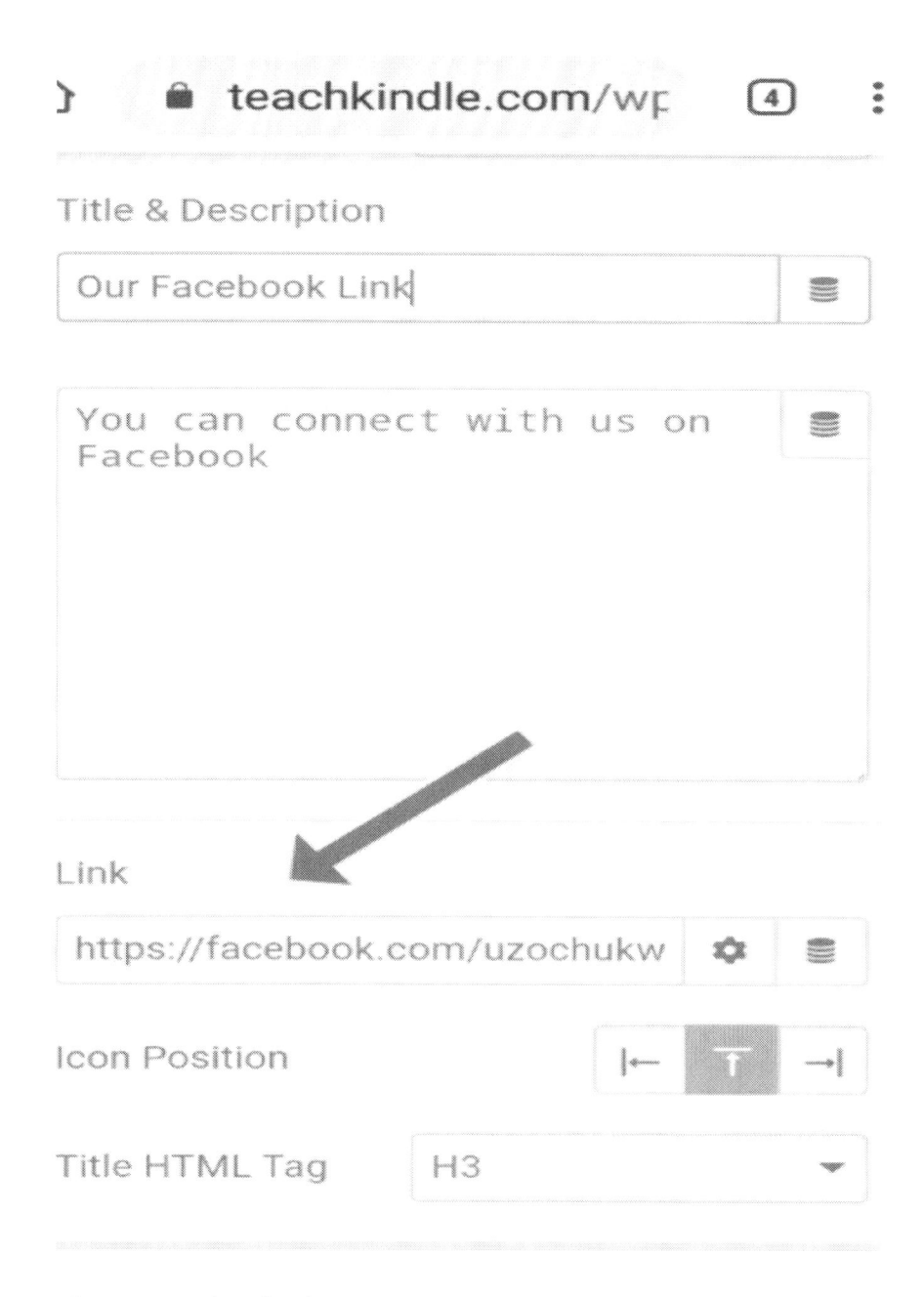

Fig 7.1.1: That is the space to add the Facebook link that will direct visitors to the page

- Click on "Update" to save the changes you made

Fig 7.1.2: Hit the "Update" tab after everything

The Update is at the bottom left corner. So, go down enough, locate it and then hit it. You are good to go.

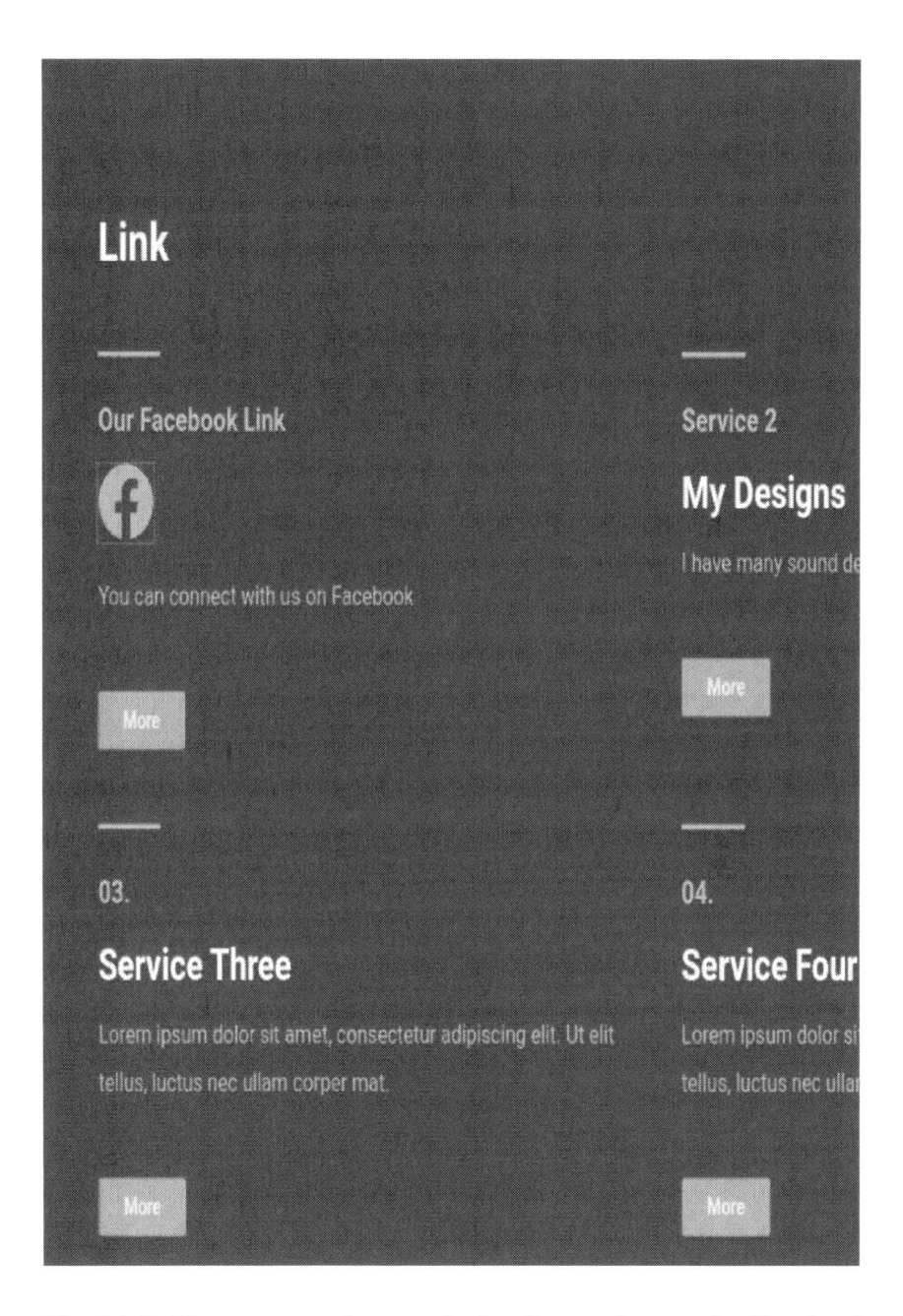

Fig 7.1.3: You can see the new look after setting up the Facebook link at the footer using elementor

The other default links with the titles "Service Three, Service Four, and My Designs" are to be worked on.

You repeat this for other social media sites you want to add, like Twitter, Pinterest, LinkedIn, Instagram and the rest. Just follow the steps I used in the Facebook media set up and you will get it right at the end.

Chapter 8

How to Build a Restaurant and Café Website with Elementor

Elementor has its positive impact in building of restaurant websites. With the help of this plugin, you can have stunning restaurant websites with classy designs. In this building I will write proper detail on how you can get this done in respect to employing elementor to do that. But before going further, let me highlight what restaurant and café website is?

What is a Restaurant and Café Website?

A restaurant and café website is that website where foods and café are sold to customers. This is a common food company in the United States of America and other countries in Europe. Sometimes, owners manage this kind of business as one in their shops. That means both food and Café are sold in that one restaurant but in different departments. And in this book, I will be merging the two as one.

I will teach you how you can build this kind of website with elementor page builder which is a plugin supported by WordPress. But in terms of integrating payment methods so that buyers can buy foods of their choice through the website, this teaching does not cover that. You can get my book on how to build an e-commerce website to read more on that. From the ideas you will gain from the book, you will be able to build a sound e-commerce site including guide on the plugins you will need to get the job finished to the end.

In this teaching of designing a food and café website with elementor page builder, I expect you to have done the following before now:

- You have hosted your domain and them installed WordPress in it
- You have installed Astra theme on your website
- You have installed Elementor Page Builder plugin and activated it
- You have installed Elementor Header, Footer & Blocks template plugin (just search for it in plugins box through your WordPress admin area, install and activate it).

- You have created your site pages and added them to the main/navigation menu of your website

Step by Step Guide in Choosing the Right Template for the Restaurant Website

There are many templates offered by elementor for website builders to build restaurant websites of their choice. Among these templates, you can choose and import anyone that falls into the category of foods and restaurant. You can use those that are free or buy any from Elementor store and use it for your design.

To design a page of your restaurant and Café website using elementor page builder, take the following steps:

- Login to your WordPress admin dashboard
- Open a new tab in that same browser you are using and visit your website (example www.teachkindle.com which am using for this teaching)

The reason I said you should use the same browser is so that the system you are using will work in a way that you are the owner of the website because you are already logged in in another tab of the same browser. That will then give you the opportunity to perform some other functions as the owner of the website or account.

- Click on "Edit with Elementor" or click on "Edit Page" if "Edit with Elementor" is not showing on top of the Page and then select "Edit with Elementor"

Fig 8: Click on "Edit Page" as Shown above if "Edit with Elementor" does not appear on the top at all

Fig 8.1: Then next is click on "Edit with Elementor" as shown in this image

- Choose the Astra symbol so you can be allowed to select a template that will fit the

restaurant and café website you want to build

Fig 8.2: The arrow points at the Astra Symbol that you are to select

- Then type "food" in the search box that shows sometimes by the right-hand side

As you type food, it will display some food or restaurant templates. Choose any from that

many that you like. You can change the background pictures later if you do not like them.

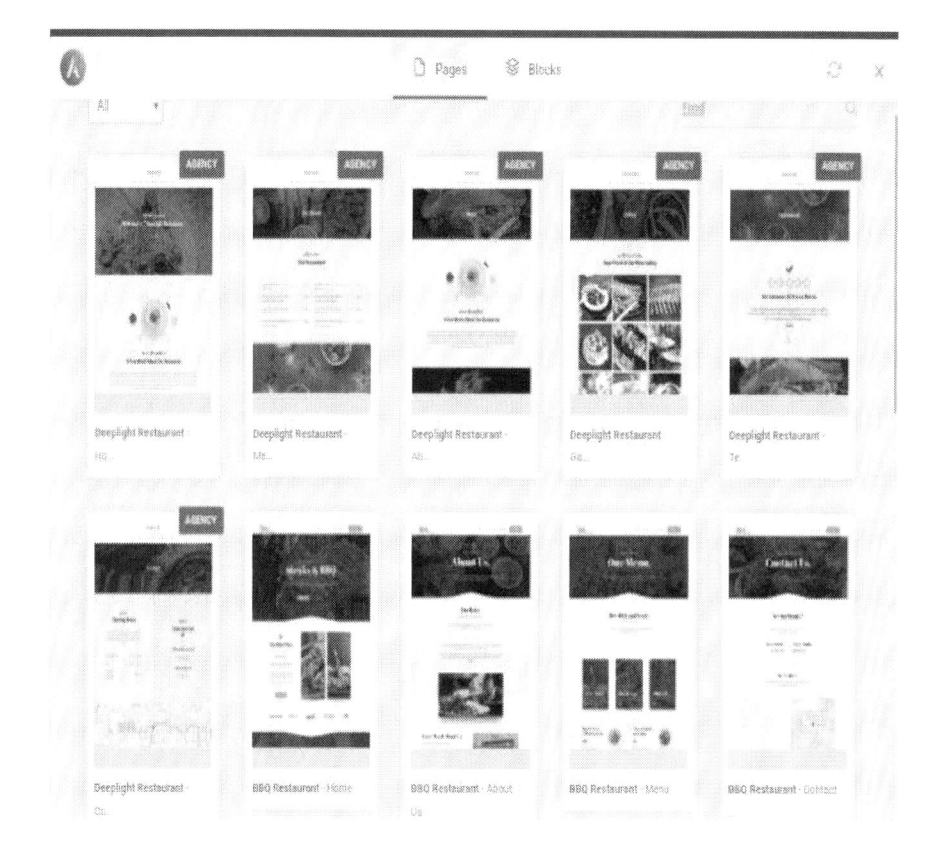

Fig 8.3: Choosing the template that will match the restaurant shop

- As you have chosen any of the templates, then click on "Import" to import it

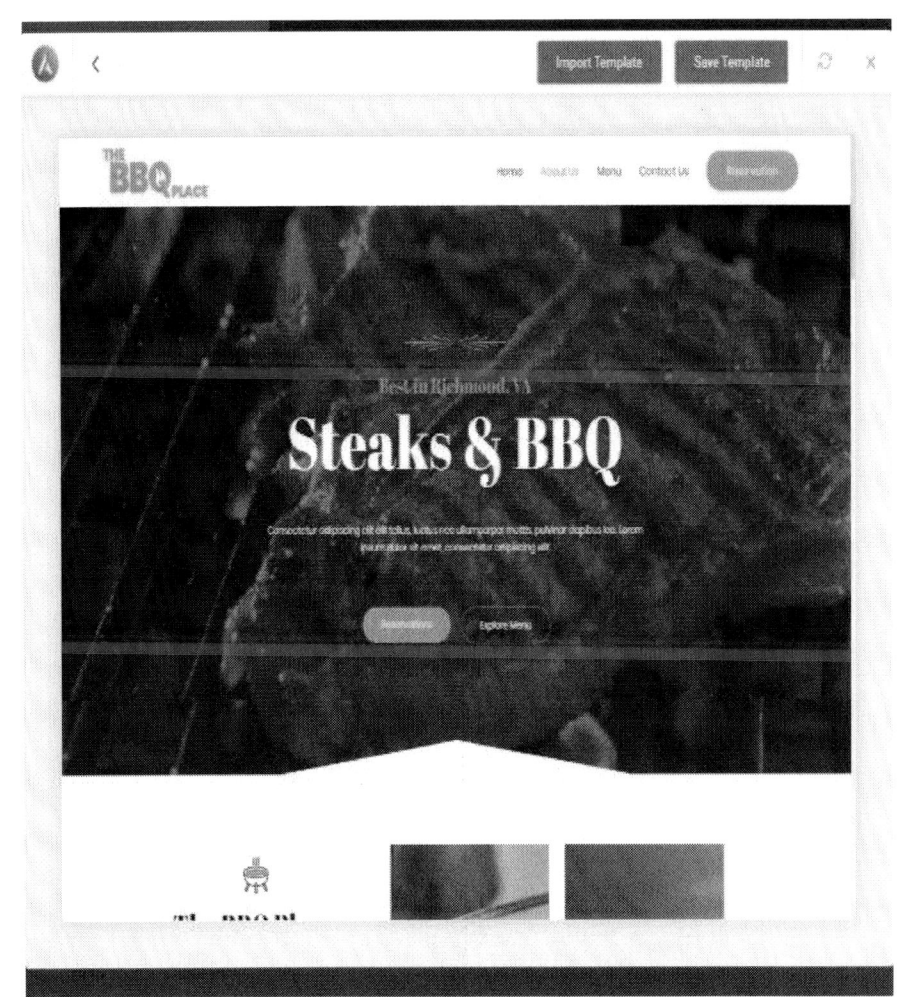

Fig 8.4: Click on the "Import Template" as shown in the figure to import the template into your website

- Make the necessary changes you want to make on the template

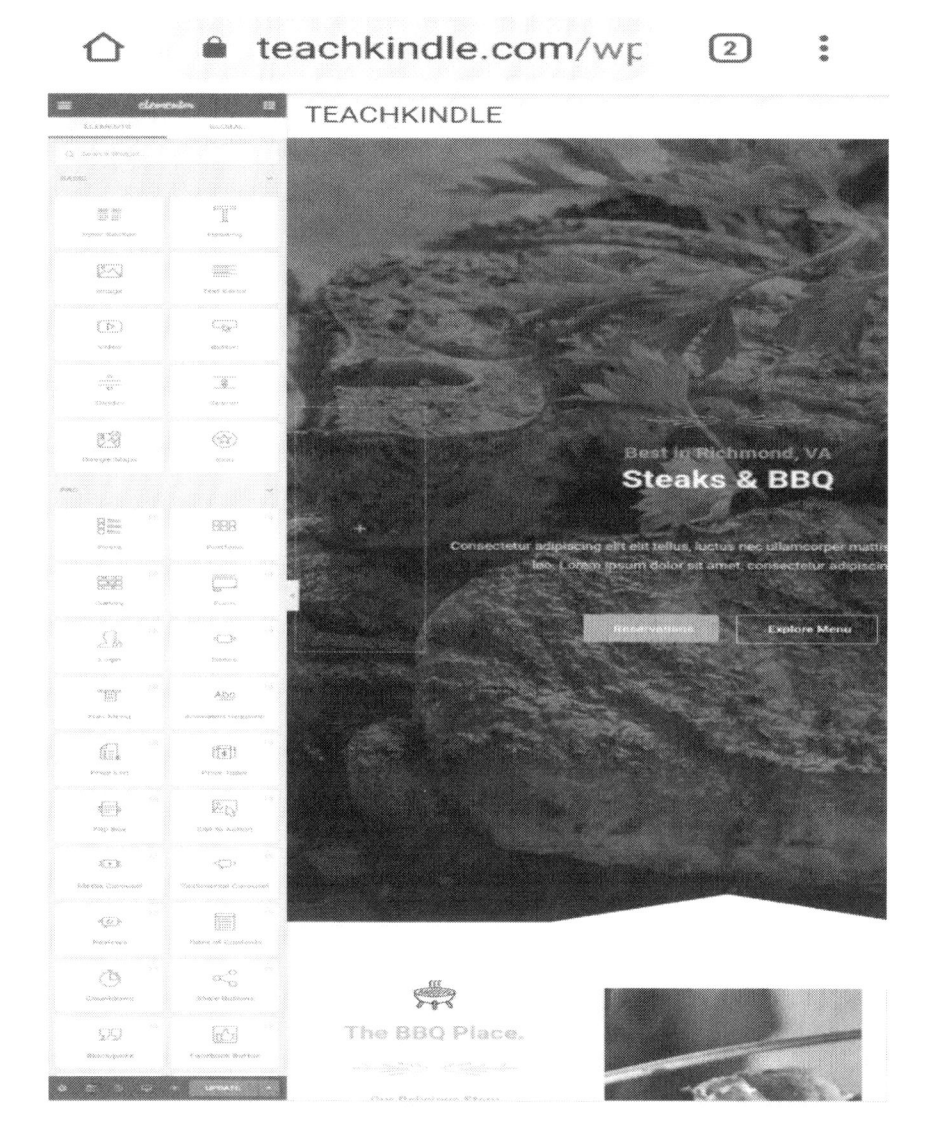

Fig 8.5: When I freshly imported my template before making changes

Take you cursor to the part of the page you want to make your change, click by the side and remove and add what you want to add.

If it is the words written on the page that you want to change, just click on that section, delete

whatever thing you want to remove, add your own and make it beautiful.

If it is the default picture that comes with the template that you want to remove, just use drag

and drop technique to do that and add the one you prefer or have in your computer.

If you want to add some links to the page, elementor page builder can still do that for you,

just add the links to where you want to hyperlink them on the page. Just have fun with the

beautiful possibilities made available by elementor.

Fig 8.6: The look of the website after making small change on the page

If you could not finish the design that day, you can come back and continue your design later. You can publish and later come back and continue building of your site with elementor. With the help of elementor, you can give different pages of your Food and Café website different designs.

• Click on Publish to Publish you created and designed webpage of restaurant and café

website

Fig 8.7: Click on Publish button to publish your page which you built with elementor

Chapter 9

Guide on how to Build E-Commerce Website Using Elementor

One of the areas elementor can be applied in building of website is in e-commerce website design. E-commerce websites in the recent time has been a point of attraction to many people. People who are running only brick and mortar businesses want to go online as they observed the advantages attached to this kind of business.

Many entrepreneurs in the recent time make more money online than how much they make through their physical stores. Many small and medium businesses in United States of America, United Kingdom, Japan, China, India, Nigeria and other countries of the world are diving into e-commerce websites. As a result of this, the demand for e-commerce website builders is of high demand. But irrespective of the fact that this kind of service is on high demand, clients will like to have well designed stunning websites to sell their goods and services.

The good news is that elementor made this possible. With the benefits offered by elementor page builder, you can create good e-commerce websites for yourself or for your clients. I will be discussing areas you can use elementor to design on your e-commerce website in this chapter. But for complete building from start to finish of an e-commerce website, you can get a copy of my book on "Beginners Guide to building E-commerce Website with WordPress". The book is available on amazon.com. You can also check my author's page on Amazon to get it.

In Summary: Setting Up an Ecommerce Website from Choosing Domain Name to use of Elementor

In summary, to create an ecommerce website using WordPress to the point we need to start building the website with elementor, do the following:

- Choose a domain name
- Pay for the domain and hosting
- Verify the site
- Login to the control panel of the domain
- Install WordPress on the home directory of the domain
- Set up the installed WordPress content management system through the control panel
- Login to your WordPress admin dashboard

- Choose a theme that suit the website which is e-commerce related and install it

In this section, I will advice you choose any Astra theme. This is the theme that works best with elementor. Astra theme is compatible with elementor page builder.

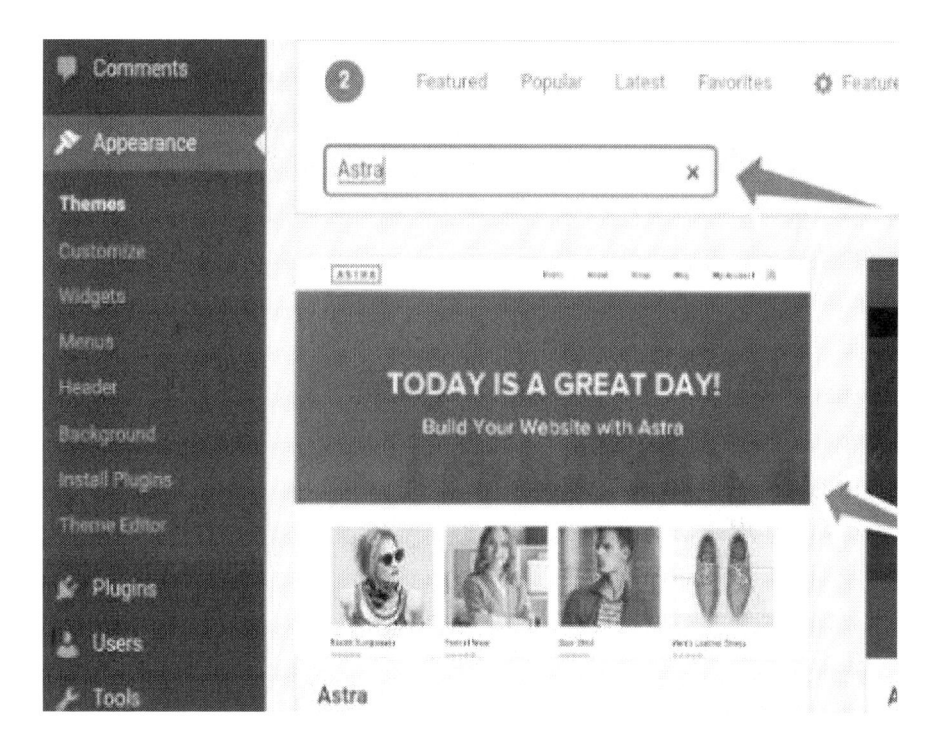

Fig 9: The preview of Astra theme when searched for using the theme search box in WordPress

- Install and activate your Elementor page builder
- Start your design with elementor

I will start the practical teaching of this section by installation and activation of elementor plugin. I will be starting from there because I will be choosing a different template which is different from those ones used to build other kind of websites. From there I will touch other areas that elementor can be used to design webpages. You will understand every step I will take in this teaching.

Installing and Activating Elementor for E-Commerce Website

The steps in doing this is not quite different from how to get it done when you are building other types of website. The only remarkable change is when you are choosing template. In this kind of website, you are to choose and e-commerce template builder instead of those that suit portfolio or blog sites.

To install and activate elementor for e-commerce website building, take the following steps:

- Login to your WordPress Admin area or visit your homepage if you already logged in

Fig 9.1: Logging into WordPress admin dashboard

- Select Plugins

Select Plugins from the list of the screen options

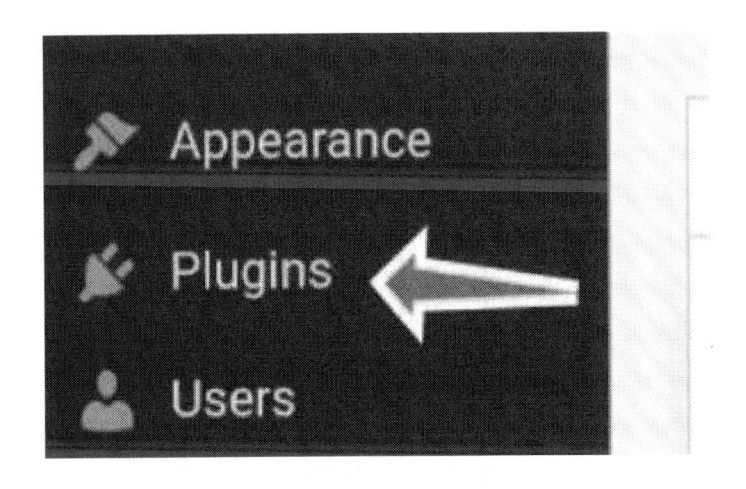

Fig 9.2: Selecting plugins from the screen options

- Select Add New

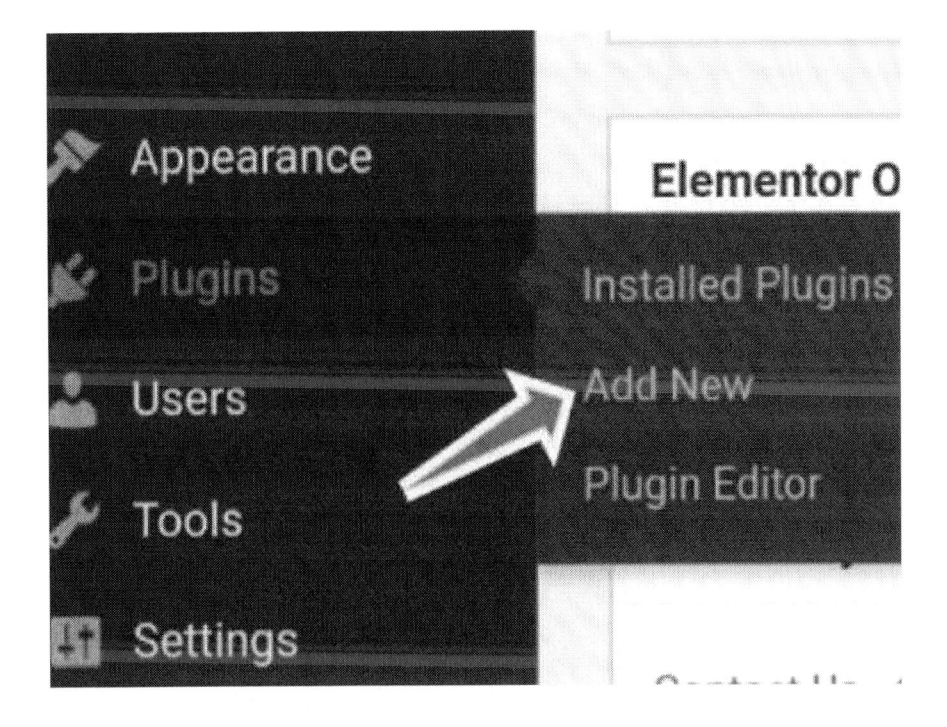

Fig 9.3: Arrow points at the Add New option

164

- Type Elementor Page Builder in the Search box that displays

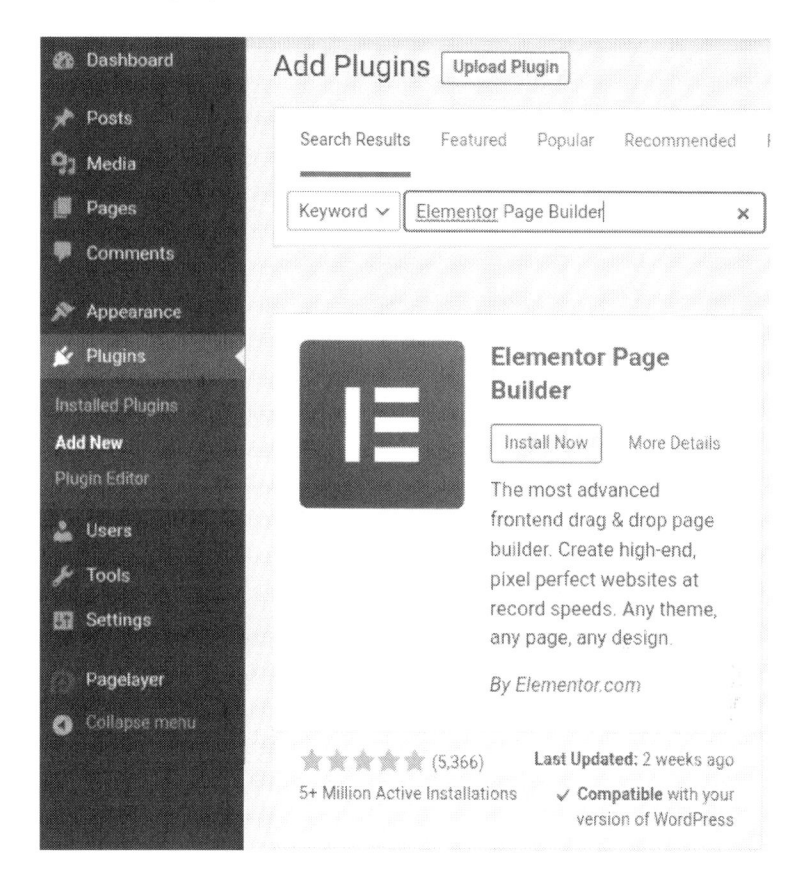

Fig 9.4: The way elementor appeared when I searched for it through the plugin search box

- Click on the Install Now button

The "Install Now" button shows in Fig 9.4. Just click on it.

- Click on Activate button

After you clicked o the "Install Now" button, a new button appears which is "Activate", just click on it and activate the elementor.

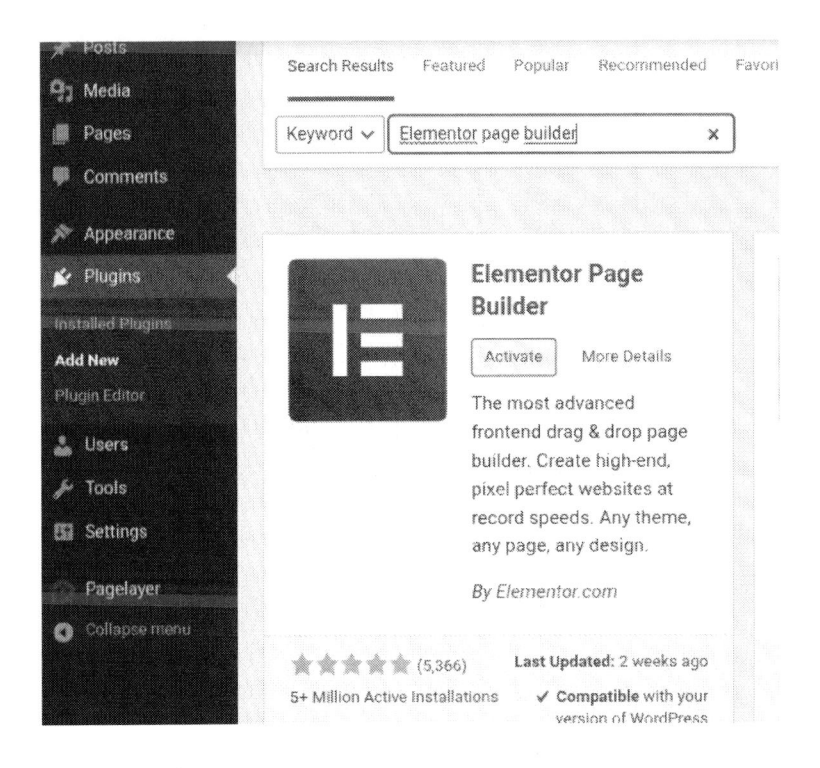

Fig 9.5: Picture shows Activate button which you are to click

At this state you can start building your website with the elementor page builder.

How to Build the Homepage of your E-Commerce Site with Elementor

To design the homepage of your e-commerce store using elementor page builder, take the following steps:

-Login to your WordPress admin area

-Open a new tab on in your browser and visit your website

As you open the new tab, just type in your website URL. If am to use the website link of the learning site am using to teach you, I will type www.teachkindle.com in the new tab I opened

-Select the "Home" of your e-commerce site

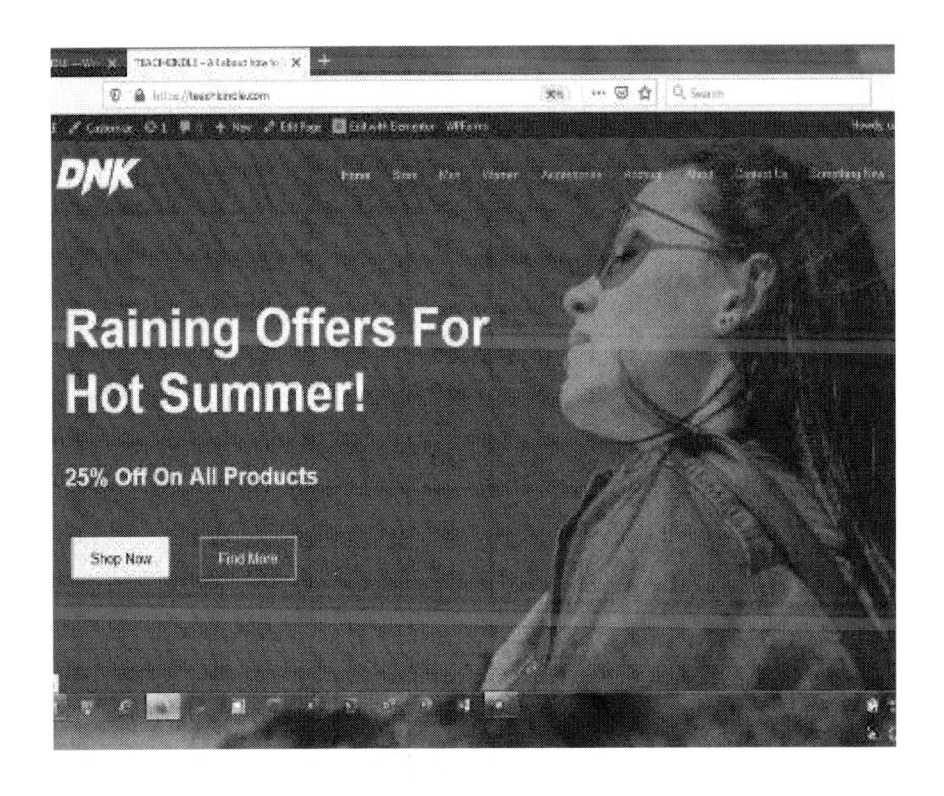

Fig 9.6: Select the "Home" menu item as shown

The Home is the first menu item as shown before "Store" and others. I selected Home first because it is the landing page of the online store. So, I want to design it first with elementor.

-Select "Edit with Elementor"

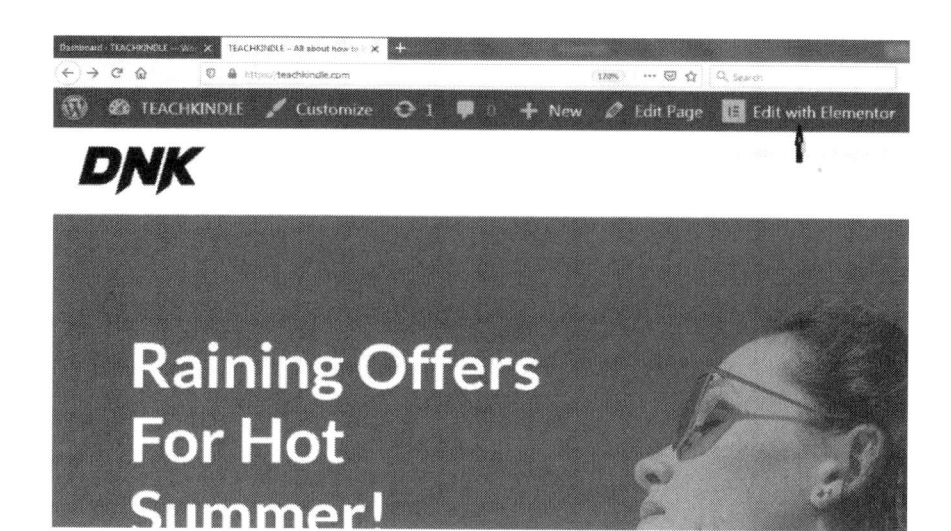

Fig 9.7: Edit with Elementor shown

When you click "Edit with Elementor", it gives you the opportunity to build the homepage with elementor.

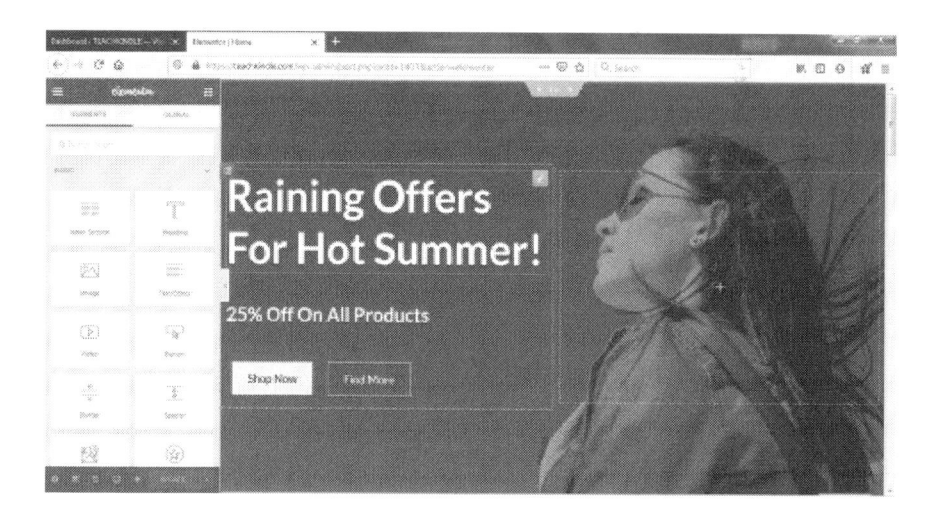

Fig 9.8: Image shows what displayed when I selected Edit with Elementor

-Make changes on the page

Take your cursor to the section you want to make changes, click on that section and elementor editing tools makes it possible for you to make changes. If you want to edit the texts on the page, just delete the texts and then type in your own words. As shown in Fig 9.3, I will delete the words that read "Raining Offers For Hot Summer!" and add my own words.

Elementor gives you that opportunity to add any texts you want to use on your website pages. So, do well to type in the texts you want your site visitors and customers to see. You can change texts and images. You can even decide to delete the words and do not have any other words inside. It is your choice to make.

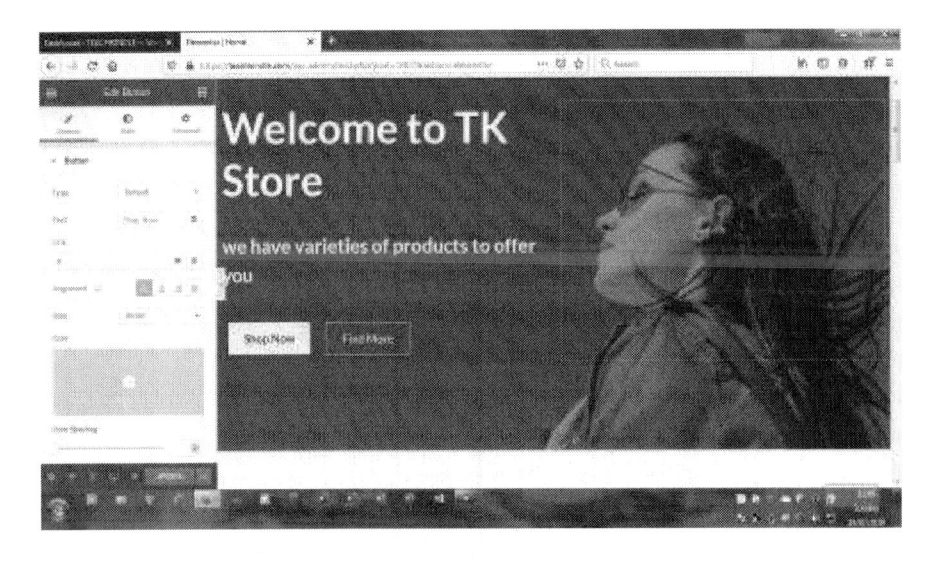

Fig 9.9: The look when I changed the default texts on my "Home"

Using the template am making use of in this teaching, you can make changes on the term "Check Out" and "Shop Now". By default, there is no link added to the buttons. So, if you are using the same Astra theme, click on the keywords, right click and select Edit. From the elementor tool section, make the changes you want. Add the link you want the customers to be taken to once they click on "Shop Now" or Check Out".

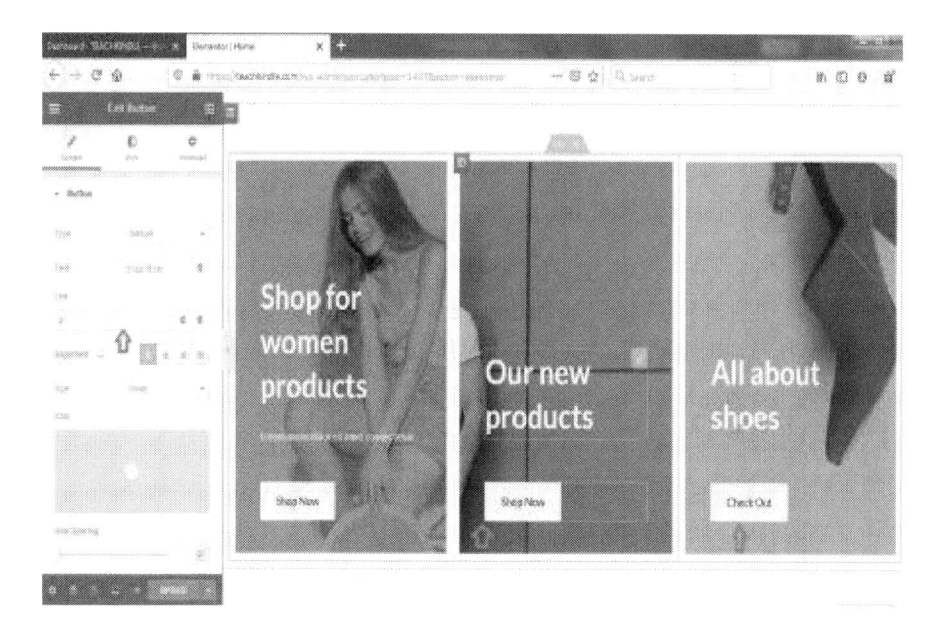

Fig 9.1.1: Inserting link to direct site visitors to where to buy certain products

You can also change the background picture by taking your cursor to the image and use drag and drop technique if you want to.

-Hit Update button

After you have made the changes to your taste, just hit "Update" button at the bottom part of the elementor editing tools.

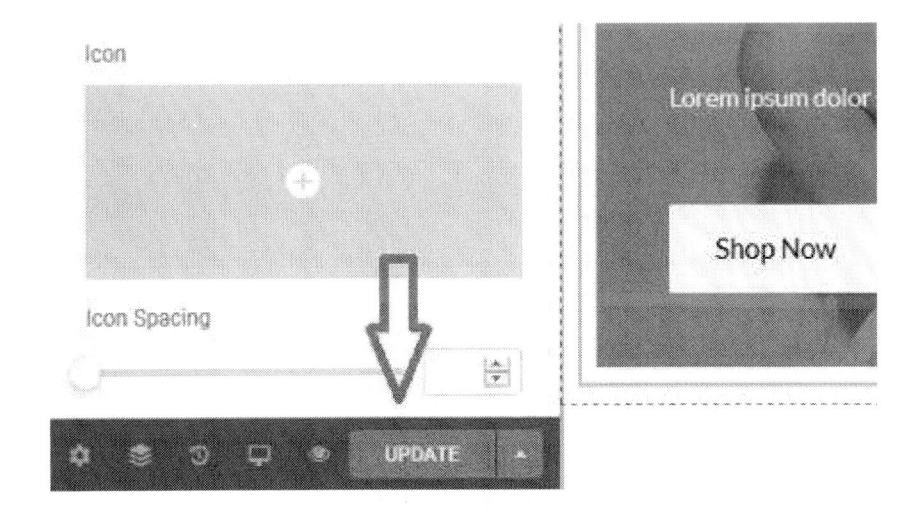

Fig 9.1.2: The "Update" button shown

Once you click on the "Update", these changes you made using elementor page builder will be saved. Do not forget to save by clicking on the button otherwise all these designs you made will just be a waste of time and energy.

With this information, you can make changes at the footer part of your homepage as well. What you are to do is to drag your cursor to the footer area of your e-commerce site and change the words or images you want to change. At the end of the activity, still click on Update to save.

Guide on how to insert or change your E-commerce Site Title, Tagline and Logo

Though elementor does not have a direct impact in this section, but I decided to discuss it for added skill in the area of website design using WordPress content management system. You will find it simple and cool.

You can decide to make your site title visible or not. But whatever be the case, you can insert title to e-commerce site through WordPress irrespective of the title I inserted when I taught you on how to install WordPress to your domain through control panel.

To insert title to your e-commerce website, do the following:

- Login to your admin dashboard

- Select Appearance

- Select Customize

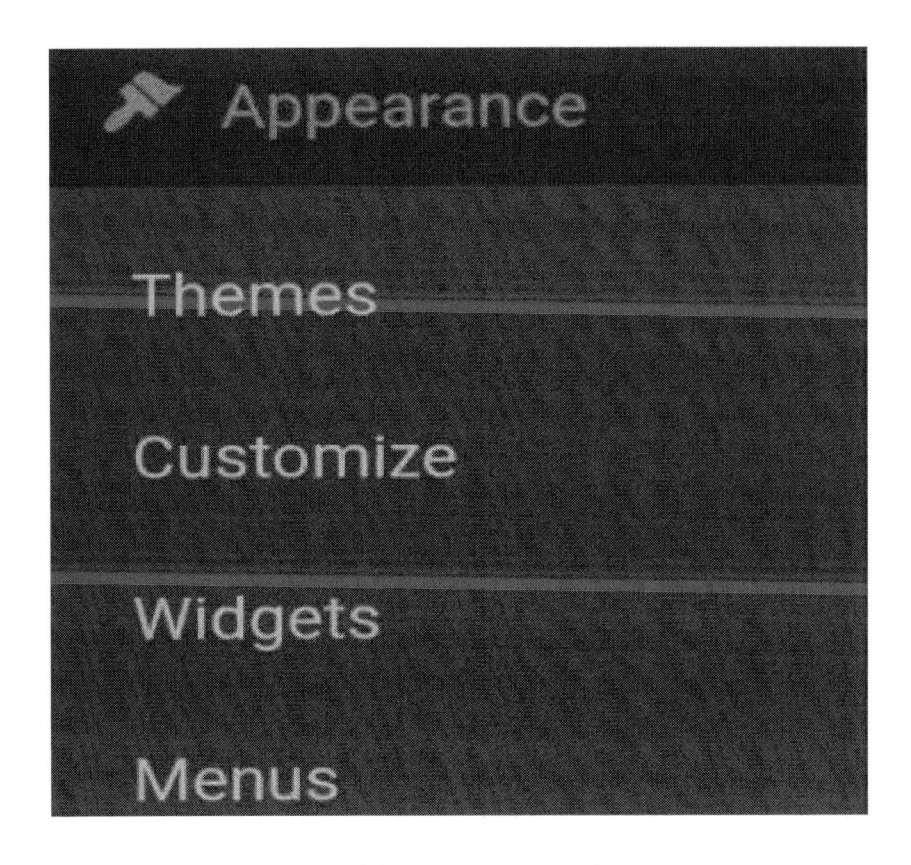

Fig 9.1.3: The position of Customize as No 2 under Appearance

- Choose "Header"

- Choose Site Identity

Site Identity

Primary Header

Primary Menu

Fig 9.1.4: Select the Site Identity option

-Make the changes needed under Site Title and Tagline

SITE TITLE

Site Title

[   ]

[ ] Display Site Title

SITE TAGLINE

Tagline

[|]

[ ] Display Site Tagline

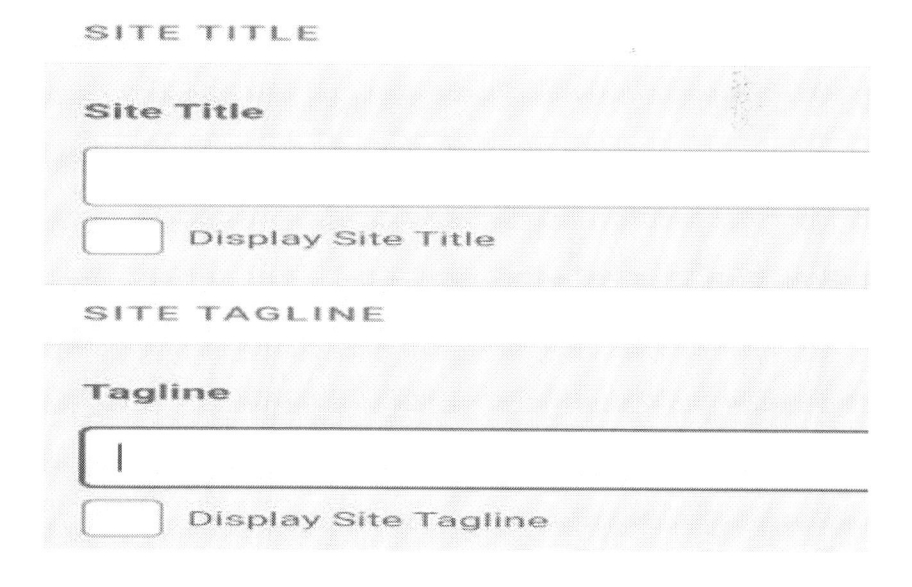

Fig 9.1.5: The boxes to enter your Site Title and Tagline

Since we want to change the website title and description, just click inside the provided space, erase the words that were there before and type something new which you want as title and site description.

- You can check/tick the box "Display Site Title" and "Display Tagline". But when I was handling this section on my e-commerce website, I decided to enter "TK Store" as my Site Title and did not tick the box to "Display Site Title". In the Tagline section, I did not add anything because I included what I supposed to put there on my homepage when I was designing the homepage with elementor.

- Change your Site Logo or Delete it

Drag your cursor up to the site logo section. You are to delete the existing default logo and then upload your own if you wish to use site logo.

SITE LOGO

Logo

[DNK logo]

[Remove] [Change Logo]

☑ Different Logo For Retina Devices?

Retina Logo

[DNK logo]

[Remove] [Change Image]

☑ Different Logo For Mobile Devices?

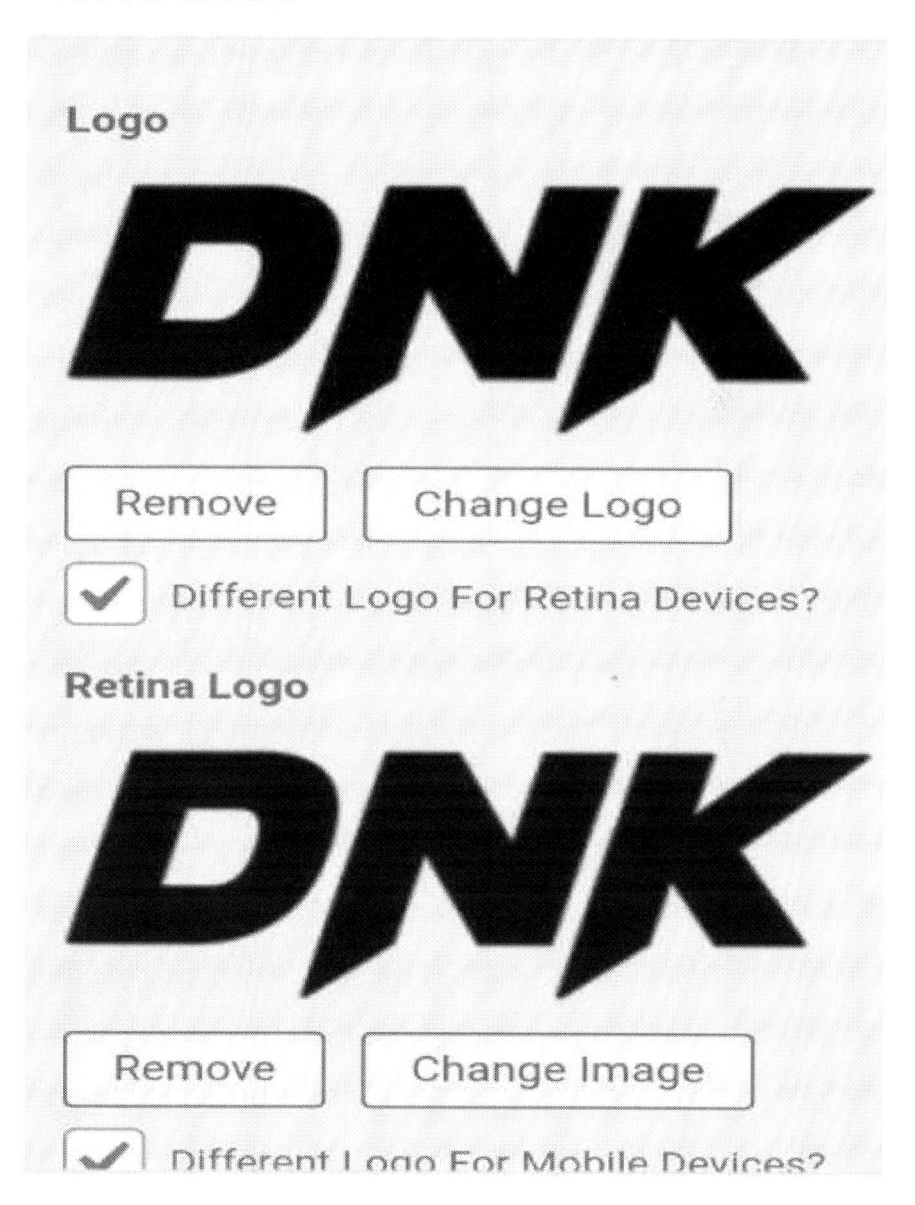

Fig 9.1.6: Default site logo on my e-commerce website

In my own design, I did not use site logo because I did not need it. I am okay with the site tile I chose to use. To remove the default site logo, click on "Remove" and uncheck the box "Different Logo from Mobile Devices" Remove all the logos on the logo section. If you have done this and the logo still shows up on your e-commerce site, then look at the instruction that may show up on top of the logo section and adhere to it.

- Click on Publish on top right corner

When you click on publish, your changes are saved. You can then take a new look at your e-commerce website by visiting the homepage.

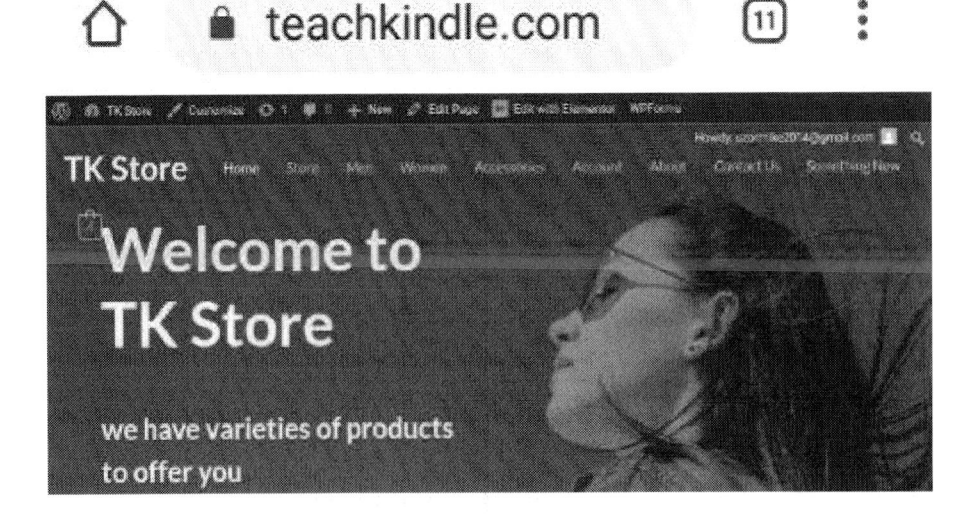

Fig 9.1.7: The new look of my e-commerce website after the changes.

I hope you understand the guide on this section. Do not forget am always available for you to write to.

THANKS FOR READING

My Email address: page25929@gmail.com

Printed in Great Britain
by Amazon